DIONYSUS IN EXILE

DIONYSUS IN EXILE

On the Repression

of the Body

and Emotion

Rafael Lopez-Pedraza

Chiron Publications • Wilmette, Illinois

Book design and typesetting by Drummond Books.
Cover design by D. J. Hyde.
Printed in the United States of America.

Cover photo: Michelangelo, *Bacco Ebro,* Firenze Bargello, (SCALA, Instituto Fotografico Editoriale S.p.A.)

Library of Congress Cataloging-in-Publication Data:

Lopez-Pedraza, Rafael.
    Dionysus in exile : on the repression of the body and emotion / Rafael Lopez-Pedraza.
    p. cm.
    Includes bibliographical references.
    ISBN 1–888602–10–4
    1. Jungian psychology. 2. Psychoanalysis. 3. Dionysus (Greek diety) I. Title.

BF175.DF466.2000
150.19'54—dc21   99–088952

I would like to thank my wife, Valerie, for her reflections on and help with the preparation of the text.

DIONYSUS IN EXILE

It is no less than an adventure into the unknown to write about Dionysus, the god of wine, madness, and tragedy, with the object of psychological reflection in mind. Furthermore, it is an adventure during which we cannot look for rational explanations. In Dionysiac imagery, we encounter a contradictory nature, we encounter irrationality, and it is precisely from this irrationality that Dionysus serves as a metaphorical vehicle for exploring shadowy areas in human nature. Let us align ourselves with T. S. Eliot, "We are not here for explanation," and proceed instead through image and the imagination.

Scholars of the classics have also stressed Dionysus's contradictory and unexplainable nature. W. C. K. Guthrie remarks in *The Greeks and Their Gods:* "The worship of Dionysos is something that can never be wholly explained." He goes on to give a list of the variety and contradictions in the worship of the god:

> its joyful and bountiful side and its grim and gruesome side, . . . the same god is hailed as the giver of all good gifts and feared as the eater of raw flesh and the man-tearer . . . he offers ecstasy and spiritual union and wild intoxication in which he himself is the leader, so that he can be called the mad, the raving god.[1]

Guthrie was addressing classical scholars, but the same could be addressed to modern psychologists and psychiatrists, who, as far as I can ascertain, have failed to take Dionysus sufficiently into account. This is all the more regrettable if we consider that Dionysus is the only god in the Greek pantheon whose attributes include madness. As a Jungian psychotherapist, I have not found any antecedent in this field for reflecting Dionysus psychologically. That madness has been attributed to a god surely means that modern students of psychology should have given it more attention, that Dionysiac madness should be at the core of the study of mental illness. As it is, our only recourse is to turn to the classical scholars, who offer a wealth of material on Dionysus.

"From the story of his [Dionysus's] miraculous birth onward, there are strange, unique elements in his myth and cult for which it is impossible to find exact analogies."[2] Guthrie is correct in that there are no analogies in comparative religions, although it seems there are some similarities to the rituals and states of possession in Corybantism, which has for so long puzzled scholars.[3] For psychologists, too, the methods of comparative religion are not going to be of help. I shall nevertheless attempt to look for expressions of Dionysiac culture in today's world.

Among all the contradictions contained in the Dionysus godhead, there is "an uncanny stillness and calm, and stillness and calm too are among the gifts he bestows."[4] Scholars have mostly concentrated on the frenzied aspect of Dionysus and have neglected this "stillness and calm," but it is a basic aspect. As we proceed with this study, let us keep in mind this gift of the god, for it is necessary to the psychotherapist's sense of his or her own body. The art of psychotherapy lies in the constellation of incubation,[5] with its "uncanny stillness and calm" so fundamental to the therapeutic situation.

It should be noted that the scholarship on this god has basically kept within the framework of ritual, cult, and the history of religion. Even so, such scholarship provides the basic ingredients for advancing a more psychological study, for reflecting the importance of Dionysus in our psychic balance, and for perceiving and evaluating the possibilities offered by the god in modern psychology.

Our first point of reference will be the myth of his birth as it appears in Orphic literature. From there we go on to discuss some aspects of his psychology: as the god in opposition to the Titans; as the god of the emotions; as the most repressed god throughout Western culture; as the god of women, of wine, and of tragedy; and as a god with a strong relation to death. Finally, we shall discuss some of the images in Euripides' tragedy, the *Bacchae*. For our purposes, we will try to avoid speculations, amplifications, or discussion of scholarly discrepancies and instead stick to the images upon which we are reflecting.

In *A History of Greek Religion,* before presenting his synthesis of the myth, Martin P. Nilsson writes, "The Orphics appropriated the earlier epic by refashioning it to suit their own purposes."[6] Thus the Orphic conception of the birth of Dionysus could be said to have given religious coherence to the scattered traditional myths. According to the Orphic hymn:

> By Persephone, the queen of the lower world, Zeus had a son, Dionysos-Zagreus. Zeus intended the child to have dominion over the world, but the Titans lured it to them with toys, fell upon it, tore it to pieces, and devoured its limbs, but Athena saved the heart and brought it to Zeus, who ate it, and out of this was afterwards born a new Dionysos, the son of Semele [a mortal, who became his second mother]. The Titans were struck by Zeus' avenging lightning, which burned them to ashes. From the ashes man was formed, and

he therefore contains within himself something of the divine, coming from Dionysos, and
something of the opposite, coming from his
enemies, the Titans.[7]

Nilsson goes on to tell us that this myth was the creation of a religious genius and remains a challenge to
the scholarship on Dionysus. It becomes a complex challenge when we take into account the strong sectarian
aspect of Orphism. We have to imagine Nilsson's religious genius as a member of a sect, with a psychology
imbued with sectarian traits: virginity, purity, "quack
diets," and "vaporous words," as Euripides put it in
Hippolytus.[8] Thus we can say that the psychology of the
sectarian was at the origin of this myth: the
autonomous, demented guilt-making of the Orphics, cou-
pled with a power drive.[9] Nilsson writes:

> It proved disastrous that the Orphics formed a
> sect from which the rest of mankind was
> excluded, and that they believed themselves to
> be better and more devout than others, for
> they had also to experience the scorn and
> hatred of the world, and what they had to suf-
> fer here, they avenged in the next life. I do not
> doubt that the important place which the
> description of the fate of the unblest occupies
> in the Orphic teaching is ultimately due to
> their feeling of antagonism and ill will towards
> their unconverted neighbours.[10]

Earlier, Nilsson says that Orphism "took place
among a people whose psychology permitted them to
react very little to the sense of guilt, and was enveloped
in a mythology which could not but be repulsive to that
people's clear process of thought."[11] We today often feel
something of the same repulsion toward sectarianism.

Dionysus and the Titans are the central characters in the Orphic mythic conception: two personified forces—the Dionysiac and the Titanic—in opposition in human nature. Thus human nature contains something of Dionysus and something of the Titans, forces that can be seen at the inner and outer levels of reality: the divine Dionysus in conflict with Titanic forces. This is the core of the myth and the most important feature for psychological reflection.

A dream has a core of meaning and so does a myth; and like a dream, a myth has a "plot" formed by the world in which it was conceived. The myth of Dionysus was one expression of the religious and mythological background of the Greeks: the great pantheon of the gods and goddesses. The anthropological and religious background to ritual and myth has caught and held the attention of scholars, and it is here that they find the ground for research, discussion, and controversy. With this background and also with the dynamism of fairy tales, so propitious for making the connections between the dramatis personae of the myth, we can obtain a better appreciation of the Orphic myth.

Before discussing the conflict between Dionysus and the Titans, we need first to have an idea of what the Titans were for the Greeks, and then to see how they appear in today's world. This will help us to differentiate that which they represent in our nature from that which Dionysus represents. It is beyond the scope of this study to go into Titanism extensively. My interest here is to bring into focus a part of human nature personified by the Titan who, in the myth, is in opposition to Dionysus.

As Kerényi points out, if the *Titanomachia,* an epic poem about the war between Zeus and the Titans, had been preserved, we would know more about what the Greeks meant by the Titans. About the poem, we do know that in it Zeus defeated the Titans by driving them down to *erebos* through the power of his lightning and thunderbolts. In *Prometheus: Archetypal Image of Human Existence,* Kerényi discusses the etymology of the word *Titan* through Hesiod's *Theogony,* our main source of information about the Titans. For our purposes, this approach is more useful than turning directly to Hesiod's legacy. Kerényi writes:

> Menoitios is an exemplary representative of Titanism . . . he is also depicted as such and suffers the fate of most of the Titans: Zeus with his thunderbolt dashes him, the *hybristés,* into *erebos,* the eternal darkness of the underworld (514–16), because of his *atasthalíe* and exuberant virility (*enorée hypéroplos*).[12]

Kerényi offers his diagnosis of the Titanic nature and its rhetoric: "*Hybristés* and *atasthalíe* are difficult words to translate, but their meaning is clear . . . they designate unlimited, violent insolence, particularly that of the Titans."[13] In another passage, Kerényi refers to, "*hybris* and *atasthalíe,* boundless pride and violence."[14] These are the two aspects of Titanism that will be our concern here.

Kerényi goes on to say that in antiquity the Titans were regarded as priapic gods. This is a misunderstanding that can also happen today. Priapus's complexity, with its strange rituals and behavior, so well depicted in Petronius's *Satyricon* and Fellini's film of the same name, are within the archetypal configuration of Priapus.[15] It is this that differentiates him from the Titans, who have no archetypal configuration. It also affords us a better idea of the Titans' "exuberant virility," which is an excess in and of itself but has none of the rich imagination of Priapic psychology.

This kind of exuberant Titanic virility can be imaged in warfare throughout history, wherein soldiers sexually possess the first women encountered from the enemy camp, a sort of horror we still read about in the daily news of the sordid and ever-present wars in today's world. However, this image reduces this exuberant virility to sexuality, when in reality it is an excessive, unbound energy that appears in many areas of life, including religion, politics, business, technology, communications, and art. The excess of the Titans, as the Greeks viewed it, can be seen in action in today's Titanism.

Further to the nature of the Titans, Kerényi continues:

> His [the Titan's] way of thinking is characterized by the same epithet as that of the Titan Kronos, who, like him, is only seemingly clever and is defeated by Zeus. Both are *ankylometai,* devious (*ankylos*) . . . a mentality which may unquestionably be called "Titanic" after its first-named representative. It implies all manner of deviousness, from lying and scheming to the cleverest inventions, but even the inventions always presuppose some deficiency in the trickster's mode of life. This deficiency relates the Titans to man and his limitations, showing them to be rooted in human reality.

> Menoitios, whom Hesiod names among the brothers of Prometheus, is characterized in the *Theogony* not only by the violence of the Titans and earthly giants. According to his name, "he whom *oitos,* mortal doom, awaits," he may have been the "first mortal." The doom that overtakes him as the son of Iapetos is that of his father. In the *Theogony* (514–16) we read: "far-seeing Zeus struck him with a lurid

thunderbolt and sent him down to Erebos because of his mad presumption and exceeding pride."[16]

The name *Titan* was not clear or self-evident to the Greeks. The Titans had no rites, no cult, and so they remained marginal to Greek cultural life with its images and forms. To us, their psychology remains obscure; we can only turn to the scholars for clarification. Walter Otto, in *The Homeric Gods,* writes, "There are many indications that (the name Titan) acquired the connotation of 'wild,' 'rebellious,' or even 'wicked' by opposition to the Olympians, to whom the Titans yielded only after a struggle."[17] Mythology can help us differentiate between the Olympians, with their many forms of life, and the Titans, with no forms, no images, and no limits.

We know that for the Greeks the greatest "sin" was hubris. We can translate the image of Zeus consigning the Titans to *erebos* with his thunderbolt as that which represents form and limits, putting under control that which represents uncontrolled violence without limits, that is, excess. The Greek awareness of the need to keep the Titans, full of hubris, pride, and violence, at bay in *erebos,* a pagan equivalent of hell, was substituted in Christianity by another sort of repression. As will be seen later, Christianity was mainly interested in repressing the chthonic gods and the emotions they constellate. In the realm of images, the repression was concentrated on the great god Pan, who came to personify the Christian devil. This meant that the Titans—who, for the Greeks, personified evil, so to say—went unchecked, and thus what they represent in human nature was no longer reflected upon and, in the course of Western culture, got out of hand.

Titanism has been difficult to recognize throughout Western culture, even today when it is present in abundance. For Plato, the Titans were an enigma, neither gods nor men, and what we might call "Titanic nature" is still an enigma, we still find it difficult to detect its presence in ourselves. Ernst Jünger brings a prophetic vision to the twenty-first century as a century in which Titanism will rule the collective.[18] There is enough symptomatic evidence in the world today—in which scientific technology, global communications, politics, and crime abound in Titanic proportions—to believe in Jünger's prophecy. The challenge posed to an individual consciousness by the Titanic collective can only increase.

There is only one extant play of Aeschylus's trilogy on Prometheus—*Prometheus Bound*—in which, with an adult tragic consciousness, he portrays very clearly the psychology of the Titans, one aspect of which is Prometheus's conversion. I see this as a mythological example of the psychology of conversion. Prometheus converted to Zeus's order but remained a Titan in essence. In going over to Zeus, Prometheus demonstrates the psychology of the opportunist: he accepted easily the rules of his enemy and tried to mimic them, but he remained psychologically within his given Titanism.[19]

The first scene of *Prometheus Bound* movingly depicts the suffering of Hephaestus as he binds Prometheus to the rock, aided by Strength and Force. Only with their help can he achieve such a task, and he says: "With heart as sore as yours I now shall fasten you / In bands of bronze immovable to this desolate peak . . . ."[20] I imagine Hephaestus as a chief of police imprisoning a very dangerous delinquent, but a chief who suffers because he senses that he is at the same time imprisoning a part of himself. Hephaestus says: "I hate my craft, I hate the skill of my own hands" (p. 22). Binding the Titan, achieved with the help of "strength and force," is the equivalent to reflecting our Titanic nature. It is not a task to be done once and only once, for the binding is a constant necessity. It alone can curb the accelerated Titanic part of our nature, to which it is almost impossible to bring reflection.[21] As a psychotherapist, it is my immediate concern to reflect on my own Titanism, which tends to appear in preconceived theories, proselytizing, techniques, manipulative fantasies, deviousness, and the destructiveness so common to human nature. It goes without saying that I must also evaluate the amount of Titanism in the patient sitting in front of me.

In the last scene of Aeschylus's tragedy, Hermes approaches the bound Prometheus as a therapist would approach a madman in a mental institution. In the ensuing dialogue, Aeschylus paints an extraordinarily vivid picture of just how difficult it is to communicate with the Titanic part of human nature. Prometheus remains stubbornly blind to his own predicament. In the end, Hermes writes him off as a hopeless case, saying, "It's plain that your insanity is far advanced" (p. 48). Then he says something that seems to me prophetic: "Now you, free and in power, would be unbearable" (p. 49). When Hermes says, "My words lead only to more words, without effect" (p. 50), it is evident that Aeschylus knew something about the psychology of the Titans. This is the sort of pitiful situation one comes up against in psychotherapy with a Titan, a supposed talking cure in which there is only a dialogue without reflection, "blah, blah, blah" leading nowhere.

Prometheus remains defiant with such words as:

Let the sea-waves' roaring savagery
Confound the courses of the heavenly stars;
Let him [Zeus] lift me high and hurl me to black
    Tartarus
On ruthless floods of irresistible doom:
I am one whom he cannot kill. (p. 51)

After this, Hermes surrenders to the impossibility of treating Prometheus, saying:

> Thoughts and words like these
> Are what one may hear from lunatics.
> This prayer of his shows all the features of frenzy;
> And I see no sign of improvement. (p. 51)

We live in a world that is ruled by a futuristic drive. Prometheus boasts: "I planted firmly in their hearts blind hopefulness" (p. 51), a line written twenty-five centuries ago that could be said to be behind Ernst Jünger's prophecy of a Titanic future. This drive represses the Dionysiac essence in humankind to an unimaginable extent. Futuristic expectancy takes us out of the here-and-now and thus out of the body—in other words, out of the time and space of Dionysus. The endless promise of a happy future seems to be the carrot that moves the human donkey of Titanism.

Titanism spans a psychological spectrum that extends from the figure of the devilish Menoitios to Prometheus and his promise of a better life in the future: two figures without forms. This spectrum is common in today's life: futuristic fantasies of happiness brought about by the ultimate in technological development going hand-in-hand with the most destructive evil. It is a vision of life in which there is no inwardness, in which people are activated only by impulses that come seemingly out of nowhere, expressed through a superficial mimesis. I consider it the task of those who do not want to be drawn into the collective Titanism of today to try to become aware of it, to think about it constantly, and, most difficult of all, to reflect on it and learn from it.

Since Freud put forth his Oedipus complex and Jung developed his concept of the archetypes, psychology has found in mythology a source of analogies for human nature. Now there is also the possibility of finding analogies in the study of evolution that may expand and back up mythological material. Hesiod, Aeschylus, and the Orphic myth provide mythical analogies to a living shadow that has no image or contour other than that of excess. But now this excess can be associated with biological impulses that developed early in the evolution of humankind.

Studies on evolution and prehistory, with the help of new scientific resources unimaginable a few years ago, have much to tell us about biology in relation to our psychic complexities and behavior. Stemming from the same longing to recreate our origin, such studies have produced results not far from what the Greeks imagined about the Titans. Colin Tudge, for example, in his fascinating book, *The Day Before Yesterday,* gives a picture of humanity's ancestors that I find highly relevant in attempting to widen our insights into the Titanic nature:

> The australopithecines were not in a general way 'aggressive', any more than a lion or a domestic cat is especially aggressive. But like lions and pussy-cats they were able to deploy aggression as a necessary technique for obtaining food. However, unlike lions and other cats which go about their work in appropriately professional silence, the method of the australopithecines was that of the chimpanzee: the creation of mayhem and confusion; the method of gang warfare. Professor Bernard Wood of Liverpool University has pointed out that the names given to early species of *Homo* are often designed to suggest that our ancestors were serious-minded people, perhaps with their eye on their glorious future. Thus they are called *H. habilis,* 'handy man', or *H. ergaster,* 'working man'. But, Bernard and I agreed, *Australopithecus hooli-*

ganensis might have been nearer the mark. Our first hominid ancestors succeeded, probably, by being at times extremely unpleasant— to a degree which, among other animals, only modern chimpanzees achieve.[22]

In stripping away the historical fantasy inherent in the labels *Homo habilis* and *Homo ergaster,* Tudge reveals a shadow that has been hidden behind creationist projections. According to the evolutionary imagination, humans became human through biological impulses and not through a well-organized creationist design. Human evolution has been opportunistic. Had *Australopithecus hooliganensis* been a skilled hunter like the lion or the pussycat, humankind would not have evolved. It was an almost boundless versatility, one of the traits of which was horrible hooligan improvisation, that made humankind. Without such impulses, our race would have been trapped in specialization; but opportunism enabled us to evolve and survive. Thus the Orphic imagination of humans created out of the Titans' ashes is psychologically not far from the evolutionists' view. This new perspective on evolution completes the background against which we can consider two miracles of human nature: *Australopithecus hooliganensis,* the opportunist, equivalent of the Titan, to whom we attribute our development as humans, and the raging god Dionysus, to whom we attribute wine, tragedy, and culture. Here we have two opposites in human nature, two different types of madness, which participate in our psyches throughout our lives.[23]

It seems to me more useful to confront a psychiatric term, for example, "inferior psychopathy," with the analogy provided by the neo-Darwinian evolutionists than with other sources.[24] We cannot find analogies for the shadow of psychopathy in what cultural anthropology calls primitive societies for the very good reason that the image we have of them today is that of well-organized and ecologically contained societies with definite form. The life we see in the big modern cities of Western society and the self-made image of the entrepreneurial hero, a boundless Titan full of pride, fit in more with the behavior of *Homo hooliganensis* than with that of primitive man.

The Orphic myth says that Dionysus was born from the union of Zeus—lord of Olympus, god of luminosity, image-maker, and joyful and tolerant father—with his daughter Persephone, queen of the underworld, she of the beautiful ankles, personifying the dark forces of the invisible underground realm of the dead. So we can imagine Dionysus as the product of very complex opposites.

Following the imagery of the Orphic myth, we are going to explore the luring and dismemberment of the child Dionysus by the Titans as an archetypal image. Dismemberment is an image of horror and a well-known metaphor for madness: in the language of psychiatry, a psyche in pieces.

It is important to realize that the myths about Dionysus move us in a different way than the myths of the other gods in the Greek pantheon. With Dionysus, our imagination is connected immediately to the most archaic complexes in humankind. We are, in other words, in depth psychology. The well-known notion that the Greeks were the most archaic of the civilized and the most civilized of the archaic has its greatest significance in Dionysus.

In the *Bacchae,* as we shall see later, Euripides gives us the crudest and most horrible imagery of dismemberment in the scene where Agaue dismembers her son Pentheus. There is also the messenger's earlier description of the maenads in the mountains tearing animals apart and devouring their raw flesh, an extraordinary picture of a Dionysiac ritual taking place in a geographically Greek pocket:

> ... But our cattle were there, cropping
> The fresh grass; and the women attacked them, with
> their bare hands,
> You could see one take a full-uddered bellowing young
> heifer
> And hold it by the legs with her two arms stretched
> wide;
> Others seized on our cows and tore them limb from limb;
> You'd see some ribs, or a cleft foot, tossed high and
> low;
> And rags of flesh hung from pine-branches, dripping
> blood.[25]

Modern scholarship has given us the notion that the Dionysiac orgiastic ritual of dismembering animals was a reenactment of the dismemberment of the child Dionysus by the Titans.[26] The myth has also been understood as an anthropological description of cannibalism, in this case, the eating of a god, a theme that has been amply discussed by the scholars on religion. The mystery of the Eucharist in Christianity is a case in point, as it connects us symbolically to the most archaic level of the psyche. So, in the image of the dismemberment and eating of Dionysus, we have a meeting of myth, anthropology, and religion. In the combined image of religion and cannibalism, it is probable that an innermost need in humankind is expressed. The image is of primal importance because it touches on a level of human nature that will always be present.

In my own experience as a psychotherapist, cannibalism has appeared mostly in the dreams of patients who have cancer or very odd pathological histories. These dreams are characterized by the eating of human flesh by the dreamer. Let me illustrate less directly with the example of a patient who dreamed that there was a cure for cancer that consisted of the eating of human flesh. The "human flesh" that the dreamer was eating came in the guise of a fillet of fish actually eaten on the previous evening. Then a voice in the dream said that people know this cure, but tend to repress it, and by so doing they are "choosing" illness. The dreamer felt that to choose between cannibalism or being ill meant a choice made by the ego, and so he left the issue in the hands of the gods. Here, one can speculate about a psychic movement revealing a complex hidden in the most archaic collective unconscious, the nighttime of human existence when cannibalism was part of human survival:

> The backward look behind the assurance
> Of recorded history, the backward half-look
> Over the shoulder, towards the primitive terror.[27]

In *Homo Nekans,* the first part of which is devoted to a recreation of prehistory, Walter Burkert discusses hunting, killing, cannibalism, and the ritual of sacrifice as forming complexes at the dawn of history and to which the sources of primary guilt can be attributed.[28] In the context of human evolution and prehistory, we can appreciate that these complexes are rooted in human nature and that the dream cited above can be seen as a movement toward survival through a psychic regression that connects the dreamer to primary complexes.

I see the clash of the divine child Dionysus with Titanic forces as a first step into a Dionysiac process of life, as an initiation, or *teletai*.[29] Taking such an archetypal and initiatory approach to this image in the myth implies that it is an unavoidable drama enacted in childhood, with all its horror. It allows us to see and begin to accept so-called childhood trauma as the appearance of the Titans coming to dismember and devour the child Dionysus.

I cannot imagine a childhood without trauma in the archetypal sense that I am introducing here. Remember that our view of childhood is imbued with worshipping the child of the sacred family, as well as with the modern paradise of Disneyland, a conception of childhood as one-sidedly pure, innocent, and happy. This archetypal view of childhood trauma goes against both traditional imagery and the prevailing trends today of a personalized and literalized view of that imagery.

(For there to be a childhood without trauma, we would have to imagine something truly horrible, namely an unvaccinated soul without defenses, without a third dimension, and without emotions—a condition that brings to mind hebephrenia or psychopathy. For example, in psychotherapy, one is faced with cases of those whose parents have hidden all that has to do with family tragedy and death. Thus there is no familiarity with serious and tragic emotions and, as a result, the person is prone to being taken over by the most peculiar and unimaginable syndromes, which include strange depressions. There is also the tendency toward formlessness of personality. Here we might consider the over-protected child in today's world who becomes a pretentious, brilliant psychopath, empty of emotions.)

It should be acknowledged that the bias toward a literalized personal and causal view has, at the very least, impeded an archetypal and historical perspective that would make for a more initiatory approach to childhood. The Titans dismembering and devouring the child Dionysus can be seen as a mythical model for a particular initiation to which the person is subjected and suffers in early life.

Modern psychology's view of the whole personality in terms of its childhood has put an excessive emphasis onto childhood. The Oedipus complex, introduced by Freud at the beginning of the century, instead of being a useful metaphor, was literalized and became a hysterical scandal. Overlooking that metaphor can be said to have started this bias.

We are following Dionysus as a god of *teletai,* of initiation, one that allows us to see childhood within a tragic viewpoint. Within those terms of initiation, it is my objective to bring some reflection to the field of modern psychology, which is plagued by unconscious projections onto and theories about childhood. Thus the archetypal Dionysiac view of childhood, with its initiatory side, is neglected or repressed, with the result that it appears in other guises. It is not difficult to see that childhood trauma has obsessed modern psychology throughout this century, having been elaborated into theories that are, finally, reductive and schematic. No new perspectives have opened up. During the last few years, the theme of childhood trauma has appeared under the guise of "child abuse," betraying a collective hysterical manifestation that clearly lacks any psychological standpoint.

Here, it may be worthwhile to look at another kind of dismemberment, that which appears in the myth of Acteon, a cousin of Dionysus, especially as it is referred to in the *Bacchae.* It is a myth that has always drawn attention in Western culture, as its long and impressive iconography attests.

> Many know the story of Aktaion, son of
> Aristaios and Autonoë and nephew of Semele,

the mother of Dionysos. It is a tragic story, and was told in various forms. According to the best-known version, Aktaion, whom Chiron had brought up to be a hunter, surprised Artemis while she was bathing. The goddess punished him by turning him into a stag, which as a rule was her favourite beast but on this occasion was her victim. Aktaion's fifty hounds tore to pieces their metamorphosed master, and Autonoë had the grievous task of assembling the bones of her son.[30]

In surprising Artemis while she was bathing, Acteon transgressed the archetypal limits of the virgin goddess. His subsequent dismemberment took place at the level of instinct: his own hounds did not recognize him. Autonoë, his mother, gathering up his bones to reassemble them is an image that makes a metaphor well-suited to psychiatry: the reassembling of a dismembered psyche with the help of the mother archetype. The myth of Acteon gives a different perspective to Dionysiac dismemberment as a metaphor for madness. It is worth noting that the story of Acteon was not transformed into any ritualistic initiatory dismemberment as was that of Dionysus.

In the *Iliad,* the great poem at the source of Western culture, Homer spoke to an aristocratic class of Greek warriors imbued with a heroic attitude to life, the complete opposite of a Dionysiac culture in which there is no interest in heroes. Nonetheless he tells the tale of Lycurgus in a way that demonstrates the psychic force of the Dionysiac myth. It is as if this myth had to be told in spite of the disinterest of Homer's audience in Dionysus. Diomedes tells the story as part of a reflection on fighting the gods. He starts by saying:

> I am not the man to fight against the gods of
> Heaven. Why, not even the powerful Lycurgus,
> Dryas' son, survived his quarrel with the gods
> of Heaven for very long. He chased the Nurses
> of the frenzied Dionysus through the holy hills
> of Nysa, and the sacred implements dropped
> to the ground from the hands of one and all, as
> the murderous Lycurgus struck them down
> with his ox-goad. Dionysus fled and found
> sanctuary under the salt sea waves, where
> Thetis took him to her bosom, trembling and
> completely cowed by the man's chastise-
> ment.[31]

In this first appearance of Dionysus in Greek literature, the blind forces that want to destroy him are
apparent, uncontaminated by the religious genius's elab-
oration of the Orphic myth or Euripides' depiction of
Pentheus as the personification of the establishment's
Titanic repression of Dionysus. In Homer's tale, we have
an image of a great god fleeing the forces of destruction
and taking refuge in his own emotions. We can take this
tale as a model for childhood: the child Dionysus sees the
Titans killing his nurses as if they were animals, an
early experience of terror in which the child sees the
destruction of his containing feminine environment. His
only recourse is to seek refuge in the lap of the Great
Mother at the bottom of the sea or, in other words, to
regress to the unconscious.

There is no more vivid description of archetypal
childhood trauma than this one given by Homer.
Dionysus crying in terror is an image of his "deed" as the
Divine Child: the expression of emotions in early childhood. The weeping of the child Dionysus reminds me of
the French Catholic writer Leon Bloy, who wrote that it
is the crying of the children that keeps the universe in
balance, thus making a cosmology, a world order, out of

that crying. He added that this crying belongs to the mysteries of the conflagration of the light, a "big bang," creating and putting in movement the whole psychological cosmos. Bloy's very poetic view leaves out any causal explanations and allows us to view the crying child in its aspect of balancing the self.

Later, in Homer's tale, Lycurgus's punishment was madness. He believed he was exterminating a vine and killed his own son, hacking off his limbs. So, although we see nothing heroic in Dionysus's behavior, we do see that he can take a terrible revenge. "In his mythical epiphanies, he exercises his destructive power from a position of apparent weakness and inferiority, as in the Lycurgus episode of *Iliad* 6, the Homeric *Hymn to Dionysus,* and the *Bacchae*."[32] The revenge of Dionysus is an element in many tales, but the creation of terror in Dionysus by the Titans is unique. Many authors created treatments of this myth. Aeschylus wrote a Lycurgus trilogy in which Dionysus is depicted as an effeminate intruder, and Nonnos recreated the tale in a more elaborated way.[33]

There is another tale that tells of Dionysus walking along a path when suddenly a group of Titans appeared in front of him. They immediately fell upon the god and tried to destroy him, but Dionysus transformed himself into a snake and slithered away into the bushes. In both the Orphic and Homeric tales, Dionysus is still a very small child, but here he can be imagined as a youth, perhaps similar in appearance to the androgynous figure described by Euripides in the *Bacchae,* who is able to protect himself from the Titans. Instead of confronting the Titans, he metamorphosed himself into a snake and thus became invisible to them. In this way, he shows overtly his kinship to Hermes. This tale supports my idea that we have an obligation to protect our psychosomatic apparatus by whatever means at our disposal. I would call this taking care of the soul, Dionysus taking care of his own Dionysiac soul. In modern psychological terminology, this would be expressed as an introverted personality able to retreat quickly into its own Dionysiac nature and there find protection from Titanic destruction.

From our study of Dionysus so far, we can say that the wealth of images he offers for reflecting the most problematic and mad complexes makes him the most psychiatric of the Greek gods. Dionysus's birth is an image of what might be called the "birth trauma." His mother died when she was six months' pregnant, whereupon his father, Zeus, took the unformed baby and placed it in his thigh, from where it was born. One legend says that Zeus gave the baby Dionysus to his mother's sister, Ino, who, according to the tales about her, had a very unstable personality. Other tales tell of Hermes taking the newborn child to the nymphs and Papposilenus, who became his tutor and instructed him in his own Dionysiac nature at Nysa. Walter Otto works out the name of Dionysus as meaning "the god of Nysa."[34]

As the son of Zeus, Dionysus is the carrier of madness. As we are going to see, he is himself both the cause of and liberator from madness: "the double nature of Dionysus according to Pausanius: Dionysus Bakkheios, who maddens humans, and Dionysus Lusios, who frees them from madness."[35] His double nature is at the core of such of his rituals as that of the maenads. This Dionysus, who maddens people and liberates them from their madness, can be seen as a psychic dynamism only perceived when expressed by an extreme image, but it can also be seen as the expression of a natural rhythm of the psyche, a Dionysiac rhythm. Ruth Padel says, "Madness is mostly temporary invasion."[36] Her work, especially *Whom Gods Destroy,* familiarizes us with madness through the great poetic art of Greek tragedy. I especially value her contribution in this respect because my own thesis is based on becoming more familiar with Dionysus's complexities, madness, and psychic possibilities. To enter madness, experience it, and come out of it again allows us to conceive of it as another Dionysiac initiation. According to Plato, Dionysiac madness was one of the four divine states of possession and considered a blessing. In the *Phaedrus,* Socrates says, with reference to Dionysiac telestic (initiatory) madness: "there are two types of madness, one arising from human disease, the other when heaven sets us free from established convention."[37] This is a very clear differentiation of Dionysiac telestic madness.

For me, Dionysiac initiations happen throughout life, propitiating constant psychic movement. Initiation and psychic movement go hand in hand. I cannot imagine that psyche moves without the trauma of leaving behind the previous stage in which it has been involved. I see initiation as beginning in childhood, as in the mythical analogy of the Titans' dismemberment of Dionysus, and passing into other initiations—youth, puberty, adolescence, adulthood, mid-life, old age—ending with the initiation into death; in other words, initiation accompanies a psychological response to each new stage in life. We know by now that psychosomatic health depends on living each stage of life psychically. To fail to keep pace can mean illness or psychic stagnation.

Much has been said about madness in relation to creation. The creative act is often depicted as coming out of chaos, a pattern found in many creation myths, and this can be seen as a regression into chaos out of which comes

creation.[38] Dionysiac madness, although it does not have
the fantasy of a creation myth that ends with a world
order, has similarities to this process. Dionysiac madness is not a mythical creation; it is a living experience
out of which comes psychical rebirth. On the other hand,
it is not too much to speculate that the energy and need
of primitive societies in the making of creation myths,
including that of Genesis, though probably the product
of a communal psyche, were the result of a psychic state
akin to Dionysiac madness. It could be of interest to compare the experience of Dionysiac madness, which can
bring a new awareness, with the madness that produces
a creation myth, wherein the tribe seeks its origins and
identification.

The insights we gather about Dionysus as both the
cause of and liberator from madness lead directly into
the Dionysiac realm of the emotions. E. R. Dodds, in his
introduction to the *Bacchae,* describes the conflicting
emotions of the Dionysiac experience:

> a mixture of supreme exaltation and supreme
> repulsion: it is at once holy and horrible, ful-
> fillment and uncleanness, a sacrament and a
> pollution—the same violent conflict of emo-
> tional attitudes that runs all through the
> *Bacchae* and lies at the root of all religion of
> the Dionysiac type.[39]

This passage is a psychiatric lesson in itself. As no one
else, Dodds shows the Dionysiac conflict in the emotion
of ambivalence. Eugene Bleuler described ambivalence
as a secondary symptom of schizophrenia. In Jungian
psychology, ambivalence is often understood through
analogy to the fairy tale *Hansel and Gretel,* in which the
two children find they are lost in a dark wood. They fall
into the clutches of a wicked witch who entices them into
her house made of gingerbread and chocolate. Many

interpretations of this tale tend toward reducing it to the mother complex, that is, ambivalent feelings created by the mother as a component in mental illness. But Dodds's passage brings ambivalence and dismemberment closer together, allowing us to imagine the internal dismemberment in a person who presents ambivalence as a foremost symptom of pathology.

Aristotle considered tragedy to be a catharsis—a purge of the emotions. In our own times, W. B. Stanford, in *Greek Tragedy and the Emotions,* says that the art of the tragic poets was in transmitting emotions to the audience.[40] It seems we have forgotten that what we call emotion came originally from the Greek word *pathos,* the root of the term *pathology.*[41] Modern medicine's scientific outlook tends to exclude the possibility of emotion becoming pathological and thus the source of an illness. This exclusion occurs not only in medicine; in modern psychotherapy, the excess of theories, concepts, reductions, and therapeutic techniques is a hindrance to the centering of the practice in emotion. The main concern in the practice of psychotherapy is precisely pathology, but it is not easy to see psychological problems in terms of emotion. Stanford, referring to Greek tragedy, an art of the emotions, complains that the scholarship on tragedy lacks a proper catalog of the different emotions, and his complaint is valid for modern psychotherapy, too.[42] We need to know more about emotions and how to differentiate them. However, there is no book from which we can learn about emotions; only our own emotional experience can teach us about emotions.

Stanford gives a synthetic view of the repression of emotion by Christianity: how the Church Fathers had always repressed emotion, centering their disapproval on tragedy. For example, Tertullian condemned "tragedy's arousal of anger, grief, frenzy and similar violent emotions."[43] Christianity was built on this repression. But at the same time, we have to realize it is not a prerogative of Christianity. Already in the fifth century, one senses a substantial gap between Greek rationalism (not to mention Pythagorean Platonism) and tragic poetry. Psychologically, repression is a built-in dynamic of Dionysus's own archetypal configuration. Not for nothing is Dionysus the most repressed god. It is as if he were a force whose repression was inevitable. Although the historical repression of Dionysus is collective, it is also individual experience and reflection on that experience that brings awareness of the repression in his archetypal configuration. Paradoxically, an awareness of Dionysus is only possible through repression, for it acts as a ritual that propitiates the god. An obvious example is that of the wine drinker who, in order to propitiate the benefits of the wine, has to control the rate and occasions of his drinking; he may otherwise run the risk of becoming an alcoholic. It is through repression that one can connect with and tame Dionysiac forces.

There is a very rich passage in the introduction to the *Bacchae* by E. R. Dodds:

> It was the Alexandrines, and above all the Romans—with their tidy functionalism and their cheerful obtuseness in all matters of the spirit—who departmentalized Dionysos as 'jolly Bacchus' the wine god with his riotous crew of nymphs and satyrs. As such he was taken over from the Romans by Renaissance painters and poets, and it was they in turn who shaped the image in which the modern world pictures him. If we are to understand

the *Bacchae,* our first step is to unthink all
this: to forget the pictures of Titian and
Rubens, to forget Keats and his 'god of breath-
less cups and chirping mirth,' to remember
that (what today we call orgies) are not orgies
but acts of devotion . . . , and that (to be possessed by Dionysos) is not to 'revel' but to have
a particular kind of religious experience—the
experience of communion with God.[44]

Dodds was evidently interested in making the mystical aspect of the Dionysiac experience relevant. One way
or another, this mystical aspect has been recognized by
other scholars, but Dodds puts a special emphasis on it.
One senses that he is troubled by the way history has
distorted and reduced its religious significance. In his
biography *Missing Persons,* Dodds conveys his interest
in irrational experiences; he obviously thought a lot
about "the experience of communion with God."[45]

As far as I know, the epiphany of Dionysus brings
about what can be called a mystical experience,
although it is very different from the mystical tradition
in Western culture's religious life. For mystics in the
Christian tradition, the peak experience took the form of
a light coming out of a void, an illumination or revela-
tion, the result of a very one-sided attitude. Some scholars have called this attitude the antithesis of God;
through ascesis, the mystic was able to wait until the
visio Dei appeared. The Dionysiac adept, in contrast,
seems to fall into a sudden state of possession by the god;
it was an emotional experience that happened in the
body.

Dodds enriches our view of the Dionysiac experience
by seeing it from the religious point of view, as "communion with God," a living religion enacted by a group
of adepts, as we see in Euripides, in the *Bacchae.*
However, it is not only in the extreme states of posses-

sion in a Bacchic orgy that Dionysus makes his epiphany. My view of Dionysus's epiphanies is that they are archetypal, and as such they are incommensurable. We can detect them in many different ways, participating in life, either enriching a personality or destroying it. Within the archetypal boundaries of Dionysus, countless Dionysiac experiences are possible.

I agree with Dodds's reaction to the way history has distorted the mystical religious aspect of Dionysus, where we find his deepest meaning and where we find a model for possession by the god. However, I would suggest that Dionysus always appears in a distorted form, that it is part of his nature. If we seek to idealize him, we are looking at Dionysus from the standpoint of a different archetype, from an Apollonic point of view, for instance, which would also distort the image by mixing up the archetypes. In other words, it would be a view from outside Dionysus's archetypal boundaries, thus disregarding the inherent Dionysiac distortion by bringing distortion of a different kind. We have to keep within the archetypal boundaries of Dionysus and pay attention to Dionysiac art to see that distortion and emotions go together. To think about emotion per se is simply foolish.

Dodds makes a good point about a "departmentalized" Dionysus as "jolly Bacchus," but from the archetypal point of view, with his crew nymphs and satyrs, Dionysus has a valid existence and a psychology of his own. Dionysus is the god of festivities; traditionally, he and Aphrodite are the patrons of banquets and symposia. A "departmentalized" Dionysus can be seen as an indirect repression. By glorifying Dionysus as "jolly Bacchus," the religious emotions of the Dionysiac orgy and the tragic sense of life are repressed. This passage of Dodds has stimulated my thoughts and makes me want to look again at the images of Dionysus in the works of the great masters, a task, however, beyond the scope of this paper. For the moment, it suffices to note that the concern of Titian and Rubens with Dionysus was paradoxical in an epoch that reconnected to the pagan divinities and yet, following our line of thought, repressed the mystical and tragic aspects of Dionysus in depicting him as the "jolly Bacchus."

It seems that Titian in his youth was driven by a certain extroverted enthusiasm for the Bacchic theme. We should bear in mind that it was a time in history when the Western psyche was bearing the cultural anxiety engendered by the inner conflict between the monotheism of Christianity and the rediscovery of paganism. Rubens seems to have brought a more complex approach to Dionysiac themes, as is shown in the series of paintings on Silenus. One senses that, in his depictions of this Dionysiac figure, he was trying to connect to something that for him was very shadowy. Dionysus seems to represent for Titian a theme that was an attraction and for Rubens a theme upon which to project obscure complexities. Their works are not the expression of predominantly Dionysiac natures, but of a historical conflict. The history of art has had to wait until the twentieth century for the appearance of a painter, probably the only one, whose oeuvre is essentially Dionysiac. There is no doubt that the art of Pablo Picasso came from a Dionysiac nature, disregarding whether the themes of his paintings had an inner or an outer connection. With Picasso, we have at last a great artist whose vision came from a Dionysiac consciousness. In this connection, Ruth Padel has written of E. R. Dodds, "his work, one foundation of modern reappraisals of Greek culture, had Dionysus at its heart."[46] We could say that Picasso was a historical necessity. From his first painting as a child, with the motif of the bullfight, to the self-portrait at the end of his life in which he reflects his own death, his work is under the aegis of Dionysus. I think now we can see the difference between a painting with a Dionysiac theme and one painted from a Dionysiac nature, just as we can see the difference between writing about Dionysus and a piece of writing with Dionysus at its heart.

These differences help us to reflect the perspective of the great scholars in relation to Dionysus. Undoubtedly, their studies of this god are full of merit, and we are indebted to their achievements. The studies of a classical scholar include philology, philosophy, the history of culture and art, anthropology, and so on, in addition to the bulk of inherited scholarship. Most of our knowledge of Dionysus comes from scholars whose formulations are rationalistic and thus far away from the archetypal realm of Dionysiac emotions and irrationality. It becomes very evident that anything having to do with the emotions is put aside.[47] For the majority of scholars, it would be impossible to live a Dionysiac life or to have a Dionysiac nature such as Picasso's, or to have Dionysus at one's heart, as did Dodds. Most scholars give the impression that Dionysus exists only in the extant Greek texts, whereas for others, and for the psychotherapist, Dionysus is a living reality with possibilities and values that go beyond the classical studies of this god.

With reference to Dionysus as the most psychiatric of the gods, we can appreciate that, one way or the other, either through built-in repression or through many bizarre epiphanies, Dionysus has a strong presence in the psyche. As we have been suggesting, Dionysiac psychology has not been studied. In psychological literature, Dionysus is referred to only rather vaguely or in short references. The impression given is one of disinterest or, even worse, of an avid Titanic standpoint that can only function through the repression of Dionysus.

Most of this century's studies in psychology have been centered in northern Europe and North America, and most of the psychologists, especially those who have inherited Jung's concept of the archetypes, have been for the most part Protestants and Jews, whose religion, education, and way of life give an ethical formation and a consciousness prone to repress or to misunderstand the Dionysiac side of life. This is a geographical, historical, ethnic, and religious misunderstanding. It is not surprising that modern psychologists find it difficult to comprehend the importance of Dionysus and his presence in the psyche. Archetypally, Dionysus represents a psychology, and if this presence is not perceived and respected, the psychic conflicts it creates go undetected. I would like the reader to understand that I am trying to encourage discussion of some of the qualities Dionysus can offer psychotherapy. In general, we are too distant from the emotions that herald the presence of Dionysus. An awareness of this distance might be the only possible attitude, for to imagine a psychotherapist who would be sensitive to the appearance of Dionysus, and who would be able to respond at a Dionysiac level of the psyche and so propitiate the ancient healing attribute of this god, is hard to imagine today. The experience of a personal analysis and studies of Jungian psychotherapy today seem no more than the fulfillment of a *pensum*. In no way can this be Dionysiac.

With the repression of the emotional Dionysus, comes the repression of the body. Ivan Linforth says that the body is always Dionysiac, from which we deduce that Dionysus is always the body.[48] This means leaving behind the intellect and being in the body, feeling the body. For me, the treasure hard to attain in psychotherapy is the emotional body, and this obviously has to do with Dionysus. We can say there is a Dionysus in one's body, waiting to be contacted, waiting to give access to the wealth of emotions and feelings.

In relation to my reflections on Dionysus and the body, there is a pictorial legacy of Dionysiac initiation rites in the frescoes of the Villa dei Misteri in Pompeii that is of special interest. The scholars have been drawn mostly to the flagellation depicted in one of the frescoes, which seems to be part of these rites. The Christian mystics also practiced flagellation as part of the process culminating in the *visio Dei*. The Christian mystic mortified the body with the idea of denying, or repressing, the desires of the flesh and the material world in order to attain a full spiritual life. It was conceived as an ascensional and spiritual ascesis. However, living in a monastic community and longing to be alone with God, which was the mystic's goal according to St. John of the Cross, mortification was in reality an activation of the unconscious emotional body, a vehicle to the mystical experience. Flagellation in the Dionysiac communities of Pompeii was part of the initiation into Dionysus, and as such it can be conceived as an initiation into Dionysus as an inner experience of the emotional body. Generally speaking, the Christian mystic's inner experience was the contemplative vision of God, but this contemplation was probably more Dionysiac than we tend to think. We can imagine that the experience of flagellation for both the Dionysiac neophyte and the Christian mystic induced a sort of madness. We can also equate flagellation with dismemberment, and in this sense it is a reenactment of the Dionysiac myth of dismemberment (*sparagmos*). In this way, flagellation falls within the framework of the divine madness of Dionysus.

Western man in particular has found great difficulty in entering the inner life. Modern evolutionary studies give us a convincing neo-Darwinian picture of how this difficulty has evolved:

> Among the many wise things that Marvin Minsky says in his excellent book *The Society of the Mind* (New York: Simon & Schuster, 1985) is that our brains are evolved organs

which have been selected to observe and cope
with the outside world and which emphatical-
ly have *not* been selected for the purpose of
self-examination. In short, we are innately
bad at introspection. Our failure to perceive
the nature of our own thinking, or the nature
of the consciousness that gives access to that
thinking, or of the words that give order to
that consciousness, are surely a manifestation
of this ineptitude.[49]

In human efforts for survival, extroversion has
developed to the detriment of an introversion that would
have propitiated increased self-knowledge and inner
vision. Such an evolutionary view helps us to perceive
our clumsiness and inadequacy in regard to the inner
life and gives a new dimension to Jung's psychological
typology of introversion and extroversion by placing it
within an evolutionary context. The extroverted tendency becomes a compulsive need for survival. It is here that
we connect to the extreme Promethean drive of the
Titan. It is no wonder that, in the face of such an evolutionary disadvantage, any method is valid, even flagellation, when it is necessary to introvert, to try to get in
touch with the divine spark within. Jung borrowed the
alchemists' term—that the opus was *"contra naturam"*—
as a metaphor for his conception of psychology.
Humankind was not built for the inner life; it will
always be an adventure for the very few for whom the
basic extroversion of humankind is both a conflict and a
challenge.

Evolutionary studies like the one quoted above allow
us to bring a wider perspective to the repression of
Dionysus, reminding us that the inner life and the emotional body are connected. From a neo-Darwinian angle,
our speculations about the repression of the Dionysiac
nature become rather superficial, limited as they are to

our Christian history and related to the dominant extroverted drive in humankind. These studies reveal the
failure of deep reflection; they also help us see more
clearly the many groups and sects that abound in today's
"age of anxiety."[50] Such sects may seem to offer an inner
vision, but in reality they are yet another expression of
the selfsame extroverted drive inherited through five or
eight million years of human life on earth.

Jung's theory of the complexes has established that
the emotional tone of the complex shows where its
pathology lies, in the wound wrought by a personal history. But we must differentiate between the emotional
tone of a complex, which allows for a diagnosis, and
Dionysiac emotion, which is archetypal and makes the
connection between soul and body.[51] But it is not only
through powerful emotions that Dionysus makes his
epiphany in the body. His ways can be subtler; he can
appear in connection with the intimacy of one's own feelings. With a great discretion, Dionysus quietly lets us
know he is just there in the body.

In the oral tradition of Jungian psychology, emotions
are acknowledged. Jung, when once asked about electric
shock therapy, replied that he personally did not need to
use it as he found the "shock" of emotion produced better results. Jung gives a vivid picture of the impact of
emotion in therapeutic practice. First-generation ana-
lysts, such as Irene Claremont de Castillejo and Barbara
Hannah, were aware of the lack of emotion in modern
culture and saw that it was often expressed negatively,
contaminated by hysteria and nastiness. Their historical
view was based on the opposites of positive and negative,
a valid view of their time. The idea was that such an
eruption of negative emotions had to be lived through
until they became positive. Alternatively, Jung's method
of active imagination offered a technique for connecting
to the unconscious. Its value was that it opened an indi-

vidual way for modern persons to "mend" the split between the conscious and unconscious. Now, within a Jungian context, Dionysus offers an archetypal approach for connecting to and differentiating our emotions as a way into the inner life.

Traditionally, among his other attributes, Silenus was Dionysus's tutor, and one imagines that he taught Dionysus about what constitutes the Dionysiac configuration and way of life. The Dionysiac nature has to be learned. We can speculate that, without being tutored, a Dionysiac nature would remain "wild" and "mad" and unable to connect to any immediate sense of reality. The iconography depicts Silenus as a middle-aged man, bald and big-nosed, physically slow and rather grotesque, a wine-drinking man. He carries very obscure aspects of Dionysus's psychology. Silenus's image is not one of Apollonic beauty; rather, it brings to mind distorted Dionysiac aesthetics. Nevertheless, it is an image for a psychotherapist interested in Dionysus to keep in mind. The usual image therapists have of themselves is imbued with a strong academic professional persona; it is difficult to find therapists who accept depression, with its slowness of body and psyche. Dr. Gachés, as portrayed so admirably by van Gogh, comes to mind as a depressed doctor able to hold and contain the patient's depression, in this way constellating a deeper level of the unconscious. I feel this is an important reflection in that it points to a possible constellation for a modern Dionysiac psychotherapy. Elsewhere, I have worked out the hermetic image of the analyst, one who is able to constellate Hermes and deal with the undignified side of the personality.[52] Following the same line, Silenus offers an archetypal image for a psychotherapist who can constellate and "teach" a Dionysiac psychology, one who can "read" and differentiate emotions. If we want to approach a Dionysiac psychology, then we have to become familiar with Dionysiac imagery and the emotions it contains. More important, we have to develop a memory of these emotions; such memory is essential to its teaching.

Dionysiac psychology is rooted in emotions and the living of life as destiny. Euripides introduces us to this state of consciousness in his tragedy *Alcestis,* when the chorus says:

> I have searched through many books,
> I have studied the speculations of astronomers,
> I have pursued innumerable arguments:
> Yet I have found nothing stronger than fate.[53]

I take the words of the chorus as being of great value in the sense that the psyche is freed of all its burden of knowledge and arguments when our complexes (in other words, our history) have become a consciousness of our destiny. For me, to contemplate the great afflictions of life (the paralyzed complexes) as destiny means a wider consciousness.

Throughout Western history, there have been many communities attached to a Dionysiac culture. We have only to imagine a group of maenads going to the mountain for a Dionysiac ritual as forming a sort of community (*thiasos*). It is the classic model of a Dionysiac community, society, or club. Modern scholarship has paid attention to this communal aspect of Dionysus in both Greek and Roman times. Nilsson, in *The Dionysiac Mysteries,* discusses how small communities kept the Dionysiac tradition of ritual initiation alive, adjusting it to the times in which they were living.[54] One's imagination is stirred by the thought of these different Dionysiac communities in ancient times and since.

One way we can learn about Dionysus's psychology and way of life is through the classical scholars' descriptions of these ancient Dionysiac communities. Of special interest is the *thiasos* of maenads, because it is the most archaic of such communities and because of the plasticity of Euripides' rendering of the chorus of maenads in the *Bacchae*. It is important to bear in mind that these were religious communities, though their religiousness had nothing to do with the norms and forms of what we call "high" religion and even less of the psychology of the sectarian. For the "worship" of Dionysus a container was needed, one in which the Dionysiac imagination could express itself fully, and the proper container was found in the *thiasos*. It must be remembered that the worship of Dionysus and his festivals were celebrated mostly in a communal ritual or in the theater.

Walter Burkert describes how the ancient religious cults functioned:

> The general lack of organization, solidarity, and coherence in ancient mysteries, which may appear as a deficiency from a Jewish or Christian point of view, is outweighed by some positive aspects with which we may easily sympathize. The absence of religious demarcation and conscious group identity means the absence of any rigid frontiers against competing cults as well as the absence of any concept of heresy, not to mention excommunication. The pagan gods, even the gods of mysteries, are not jealous of one another; they form, as it were, an open society.[55]

This is an illuminating passage that makes us think about the possibilities of imaginative freedom in such religious communities.

Let us to take a brief look at how Dionysiac religious worship survives in today's world indirectly through Dionysiac art forms and syncretism in Christianity. My interest is to see how the Dionysiac way of life is lived in small communities today, communities in which the psychology of the *thiasos* is a living reality.

In Andalusia, culturally the oldest part of Spain, the Andalusians live the syncretism of their culture and enrich their lives with two very strong Dionysiac art forms: the refined and emotional art of bullfighting, developed patiently down the centuries from the ancient ritual of killing the bull, and flamenco song, guitar, and dance. Death maintains a strong presence in both.

The *thiasos* affiliated with bullfighting are called *peñas* and *tertulias* (clubs) in which a group of aficionados gather around the name of their favorite bullfighter. One senses that there is a bit of the old worship of the hero as killer of the bull, or of archaic sacrifice, but, at the same time there are a lot of culturally sophisticated conversations, discussions, and lectures concerning the history and art of bullfighting. When the aficionados talk about bullfighting and bullfighters in their *peñas* and *tertulias,* they are making an indirect, though very real, connection to the primordial image of sacrificing the bull, with its strong Dionysiac imagery. Through this indirect mode, the members of the *peñas* and *tertulias* keep their imaginations alive with the help of a Dionysiac art form: the emotion engendered by the beauty of the fighting bull, the constant risks taken by the bullfighter, the memory of great *faenas,* and the deaths of famous bullfighters.

The historical origin of the present form of flamenco is uncertain. Historians of flamenco cite many strands that went into the making of this art: ancient Greek, Roman, and Jewish laments, Moorish elements, and, most important, the contribution of the gypsies. Flamenco has integrated all these elements and continues to display its Dionysiac capacity to integrate different cultural influences. These varied strands reveal the many levels that compose the Andalusian collective unconscious. J. M. Caballero Bonald notes, "The Andalusian possesses an astonishing capacity to assimilate diverse outside influences, transforming them over time into authentic manifestations of their own ancestral culture."[56]

The *juerga* is the most Dionysiac expression of all. It consists of a group (a *thiasos*) of flamenco singers and aficionados singing for days, waiting for the *duende* to appear, waiting for the emotion propitiated by the music. It happens when some mysterious quality in the song strikes the group simultaneously. One can say it is an emotion that arises out of the mystery of Dionysiac aesthetics.

The emotions expressed in all flamenco songs range from the most apparently superficial to the most complex and profound. The catalogue of different styles displayed in this genre of music is impressive, ranging from the light *sevillanas,* to the very dark *tonás, martinetes, seguiriyas,* and *peteneras.* The wide range contained within flamenco shows the wealth of Dionysus's possibilities and points to a Corybantic differentiation in which one finds the music akin to one's own psychology.[57]

The same communal Dionysiac feeling can be found in the *cofradías* (confraternities, associations). These associations are attached to the parish churches in Andalusia and devoted to a specific image, especially one of the many Virgins created by the Andalusian imagination, as well as to images of the Passion and Crucifixion of Christ. Such images are central to the processional rituals of the Catholic Church during Easter, but in Andalusia one can perceive the Christian tradition combined with the unique flamenco ingredient of the *saeta,* an unaccompanied voice singing to an image while the procession halts until the song is finished. One can see here a syncretism in which a strong Dionysiac emotion prevails. This syncretism with Christianity goes even further: in relatively recent times, the Rociera Mass has gained popularity in Spain. It comprises a style of flamenco singing attached to the worship of the Virgin of Rocio. The singing of the Rociera gives to the ritual of the Mass an emotion, reminding us of the use of spirituals in the religious practices of the North American black community.

In flamenco and bullfighting, we can perceive the presence of strong Dionysiac forms of art.[58] However, I am aware that such art forms may be difficult for some of my readers to accept. Not everyone can endure the unaccompanied flamenco song called the *martinete,* an experience which, incidentally, makes me think of the mythological contest between the Dionysiac musician Marsias and Apollo, exemplifying two different ways of feeling and expressing music. Likewise, in the color and beauty of the bullfight, not everyone can endure the killing of the bull. It can provoke repulsion, but repulsion, too, is part of the Dionysiac experience.

There is more to say in relation to Dionysus and music. The Greeks praised the choral music of the tragic plays as the greatest form of their art, but unfortunately we know next to nothing about this Dionysiac music. In the ample iconography of the satyrs, those strange creatures with animal characteristics, the members of a Satiric chorus wore masks and played musical instruments such as the lyre, the pipe, and the flute. One wonders what sort of music they played; it probably aroused the same sort of emotion we experience when hearing the Mediterranean pipes and flutes played in today's festivals.

Here jazz, another Dionysiac form of music, comes to mind. Jazz began as the musical expression of an oppressed minority, the descendants of the American black slaves, and developed its basic form in New Orleans. It was an improvised music, played after funerals, with a strong rhythm, expressing emotion and creating a Dionysiac consciousness of death. Modern jazz was born from this Dionysiac beginning; it developed and went on to achieve universal recognition. For me, jazz has been a great epiphany of Dionysus in this century. Its early beginnings evoke an image of a modern expression of the Dionysiac satyrical music of ancient times.

What the satyrs represented in the Dionysiac Greek imagination poses something of a challenge for both scholars and psychologists. Scholarship on the satyrs has been schematic, giving little food for psychological insights. In contradistinction to the maenads who were also part of Dionysus's retinue, they are usually depicted as all having the same characteristics: Silenian faces, long hair, pointed ears, and horsetails, playing their musical instruments, displaying lascivious behavior, and drunk on wine. It is obvious that they represent a connection to the animal realm in humans, and they must also represent an important side of Dionysus, an animal side that can be lived and can have meaning within his archetypal boundaries.[59] The *thiasos* of satyrs makes one think of modern carnival societies in which the members' dress and makeup are identical, in which the person's individuality is hidden behind a mask and so gives license to indulge in all kinds of normally unacceptable behavior.

Nowadays the word *satyrical* is used in connection with literature and theater to denote the art of diminishing a subject by making it ridiculous, evoking amusement, contempt, and scorn. Thus it differs from comedy, which evokes simple laughter, in that it is derisive and used more as a weapon. Dionysus is the god of comedy as well as tragedy.

There are no extant Greek satyr plays, but there is the magnificent fragment that Euripides introduces in *Alcestis,* providing an image of satyrical psychology in action. Heracles, who is on his way to Thrace to negotiate a deal for a horse with Diomedes, arrives at Admetus's house just as the funeral of Alcestis, the wife of Admetus, is taking place. Combining the hero and the satyrical fool, he boldly goes down to the realm of the dead to bring Alcestis back to her grieving husband. Euripides uses this satyrical handling of death as a resource in his own work—a tragedy.[60] His portrayal of the foolish Heracles dealing easily in the realm of the dead is the best example we have of the possibilities of expression in a Greek satyrical play. We can imagine that the attitude toward death in these plays expressed a clowning, mocking, foolish aspect of Dionysus.[61] This satyrical handling of death through the foolishness of the hero could provide a very flexible imagination for keeping death in the here and now of life. Today the prevalent attitude is mirrored in the line Aeschylus put into the mouth of the Titan Prometheus: "I caused men no longer to foresee their death" (p. 28).

There is something else to consider about the satyrs: the archetypal nature of a personality can be detected through that person's physiognomy; a "child" of Artemis, or of Hestia, or of Aphrodite, for example, has her own specific physiognomy and way of being. I tend to think that the band of maenads and satyrs accompanying

Dionysus can be taken as the image of the archetypal children of the god.

My interest in the above has been to show how the Dionysiac culture is lived and expressed in small communities and historical "pockets," whether they be in Greece, Pompeii, Andalusia, or New Orleans, and to propitiate an indirect learning about the Dionysiac way of expression in different cultures that otherwise might go unrecognized. Psychology, with its interest in societies and institutes, might consider the many possibilities offered by the group formation of the *thiasos*.

Dionysus was mostly worshipped by women. Their worship seems to have been an orgiastic religious experience, that "communion with God" mentioned by E. R. Dodds. Although we do not really know what Dionysiac enthusiasm meant to those Greek women, we can ask ourselves just how the cult nourished them through its mystery and ecstasy. We can imagine that the souls of those women were replenished by the Dionysiac experience and that it probably provided them with insights beyond our imagination today. The mysteries give the soul a dimension of living religious experience which, in the case of Dionysus, means feeling oneself in the body, in the specific emotion of the moment. We have some notion of what Dionysus might have meant for the Greek women when we see his epiphany in the psyches of modern women.

Let me illustrate this with two dreams of a fifty-two-year-old Venezuelan woman, married, with three children, whose life was dedicated to the home. In her initial dream, she was in a desert with only a small jug, half-filled with water, a little bit of water that wouldn't last long. This dream demonstrates a psyche in a very precarious state. In her second dream, she is dressed in white and dancing barefooted in ecstasy for miles and miles. This is a very precise image of a maenad. The word *maenad* comes from *mania,* meaning in this context a state of possession. Jane Ellen Harrison says, "Their name . . . represents a state of mind and body."[62] I understand this dreamer's psyche as being thirsty for Dionysus. Out of her suffering comes a Dionysiac experience as the remedy for her dryness and desolation. It seems that, through Dionysus, through a corporeal realization in which the god provides an ecstatic experience, a woman connects to her suffering. I consider there to be a very important difference between connecting to one's suffering and suffering in itself.

There is some confusion between the Dionysiac experience and hysteria. For example, Dodds, who was interested in states of possession, mentions in *The Greeks and the Irrational* the two catalogues of states of possession in ancient times, the one of Hypocrates and the other of Euripides. He also worked out the states of possession in Corybantism, but in his appendix on maenadism he gives the impression that he sees Dionysiac possession as a container for hysteria: "what the *Bacchae* depicts is hysteria subdued to the service of religion."[63] For me, this is a way of seeing maenadism that pertains directly to psychotherapy. By channeling hysteria into the container of an organized religious rite every two years, the Dionysiac cult kept it within bounds and gave it a relatively harmless outlet. Nevertheless, it is necessary to differentiate Dionysiac possession from hysteria, because they are two different states. A dancing maenad is possessed by Dionysus's divine madness, not by a contagious hysteria. As Niel Micklem shows in his book, *On the Nature of Hysteria,* hysteria has to do with different complexities.[64] Actually, hysteria is a lack of body, whereas Dionysiac possession is a unique body experience, as the second dream of the Venezuelan woman above shows. But we can add, following Micklem, that hysteria, being archetypal too, is always there and always capable of manifestation.

The relationship between Dionysus and Ariadne tells us more about what the god meant to Greek women. The Greek imagination reached its highest level of projection by equating the couple Dionysus and Ariadne with Eros and Psyche. For the psychological implications of the relationship, we need to trace Ariadne's family origins. Her mother was Pasiphae, the Queen of Minos, and her sister was Phaedra, who became a tragic figure. The tragic family history began with Pasiphae's bestial copulation with a bull, which resulted in the birth of the Minotaur. This monstrous offspring was kept at Minos in the labyrinth constructed by Daedalus, where, once a year, youths and maidens were sacrificed to him. It was Ariadne who gave Theseus, the hero who set out to kill the Minotaur, the thread with which he could find his way out of the labyrinth. The Minotaur in the labyrinth makes for an image of negative feelings and fantasies that can flood the psyche emotionally in a destructive way. Ariadne had the wisdom to use the hero for the task of killing her half-brother, the Minotaur, what the psychologist would call a transformation of the negative feelings and fantasies of an inherited history (symbolized by the Minotaur and the labyrinth) and their integration into the personality through the intervention of the feminine.

After the killing of the Minotaur, Theseus and Ariadne left for Athens, stopping off at the island of Naxos. What happened there has been an inspiration for poets and musicians. Ariadne fell into a sort of trance, and Theseus left her there on the beach and went on to

Athens. Then Dionysus appeared to Ariadne and made her his wife. He is probably the only god who maintained a monogamous relationship, and I would guess that this was how Greek women imagined him. In looking at his marriage a little closer, we can speculate that Dionysus married a woman who had integrated her negative feelings and fantasies through the killing of the Minotaur, and she was thus a suitable spouse for Dionysus. A Dionysiac relationship would presuppose that it carries both positive and negative feelings together, or, to put it another way, that the relationship contains the madness of ambivalence in the assimilation of both positive and negative attitudes. The tales about Ariadne say that she died in travail, thus drawing her further into the tragic Dionysiac cycle. Perhaps this part of the tale was an imaginative homage made by the Greek women of ancient times to all women dying in travail.

As far as I am concerned, the only really new thing to have happened in the history of humankind is the extraordinary leap forward made by women in recent times, moving as they have, in a very short time, into fields that were previously the prerogative of men. In today's universities, the numbers of women students are higher than those of men, creating a situation that would have been unthinkable a few years ago. However, in achieving acceptance and success in academic, scientific, political, and business life, they have joined the Titanic side of history, with its excess of technological, political, and entrepreneurial aspects of life.

We have to question the one-sided characteristics shown by this new successful Titanic woman. Perhaps the image of a maenad in the *Bacchae,* who worshipped Dionysus in ancient times and who was left behind by history, is still lurking somewhere in the unconscious psyche and merits reflection. It is hard to imagine how

this suppressed maenad, or the psychology she personifies, behaves within the complexities of modern woman.
We can see that the instrument modern women use
to meet the challenge of their leap forward is Titanic
acceleration. Terms such as *hysteria* and the *pseudo
logos* of animus come to mind as complements of this
acceleration.[65] The body has only the physical fitness of
the virginal Artemis—achieved through jogging, aero-
bics, dance, and so on—to sustain it. But on no account
should a gymnastic Artemisian body be confused with a
Dionysiac emotional body.

There is much discussion in meetings of gynecolo-
gists, internists, endocrinologists, and psychiatrists on
the psychosomatic tendencies found in modern accelerated women with their many new responsibilities.
Among those psychosomatic conditions, just to mention
one ailment, thyroid problems have reached epidemic
proportions.[66] No one knows exactly in what way women
today are paying for their historical leap forward, but in
psychotherapy it is common to meet women who are
actually "dismembered" by their drive to study, compete
in the workplace, and be a mother to their children. It is
valid to take an evolutionary view of this way of life and
posit that women's biology is not "programmed" for it.
There is a wide biological gap.

The Orphic tale in which Dionysus was born the son of
the Olympic god Zeus and Persephone, queen of the
underworld, was probably behind Heraclitus's fragment:
"Dionysus and Hades are one and the same," an asser-
tion that strongly connects Dionysus to death. We can
imagine different ways of conceiving death and its

47

meaning within the different archetypal realms of the gods and goddesses. In the case of Dionysus, death has an immediacy: it is lived in the present, in the here and now; its presence in the imagination and the emotions nourish the soul. Death is the strongest emotion and the most individual. I would like to mention here the difference between the outwardly expressed emotions of pain and grief at the death of a loved one and the inwardly felt emotions when contemplating one's own death.

My intention is not to contradict the scholars who have worked on Dionysiac rites of death. Their evidence is based mostly in the culture of sarcophagi, with its imagination of an afterlife. They tell us that in Greek and Roman times there were Dionysiac societies that had a mourning ritual for the death of members. From the standpoint of psychology, one can view this imagination as a way to feed the ritual of death in the *thiasos* and to propitiate the Dionysiac emotion of death: the here and now of death. As Susan Guettel Cole writes: "When worshippers pray to Dionysus for safety or preservation, their prayer refers to this life, not the next."[67] Her analysis of an inscription in which appears the word *save* implies a connotation of protection and preservation. *Salvation* is a term that belongs to the rhetoric of the Titans, a rhetoric that I worked out in relation to Don Juan in *Hermes and His Children*.[68] Salvation is also a tenet of Christianity and the central attraction in modern sects, something to be taken into consideration when such fantasies appear in psychotherapy.

In today's world, it is apparent that death has lost its former place in life. Embarrassment in the face of death is commonplace. The Dionysiac rites of death have been lost and have fallen into the hands of Dionysus's opposite—the Titans. Let us remember again what Prometheus claimed: "I caused men no longer to foresee their death" (p. 28). From the Middle Ages on, death has faded in its coloring of life. Generally speaking, death has become just a word, detached from the image that gives it emotion. In the Catholic tradition, there remains some imagery of death. Alfred Ziegler refers to the baroque imagery of death in relation to psychosomatic medicine and psychotherapy in a note under the illustration of the baroque relics of St. Felix: "The worship of the bones of martyrs is not only of religious import but is related to the medical theory according to which similars are treated with similars, similis simile."[69] He saw this connection to death in the preservation of relics, but I see a connection also in terms of the processional images of the passion and agony of Christ. The image of agony propitiates an access to death. Agony is an inner image in daily life, notwithstanding the causes of illness or any direct association. Being an image, it is not just a word; it has its own psychology. In not acknowledging it as a psychological reality, modern medicine has destroyed the possibility of a consciousness of agony. When a patient begins to agonize, the physician invariably prescribes a pill to soothe the passage.

In relation to Dionysus and death, besides the already mentioned fragment of Heraclitus, there is Greek imagery of the underworld's main deities. A Greek vase painting depicts Demeter, Hermes, Persephone, and Dionysus, and we can imagine a chthonic trinity of Hades, Pluto, and Dionysus, representing respectively death, wealth, and tragedy and culture, enriching our view of the underworld level of the psyche.[70] If Dionysus has a close connection to death, then it follows that he has a close connection to depression. Traditionally, Saturn, the old Kronos, is the figure that has most often caught the imagination in relation to depression. The iconography depicts Saturn as a cripple with his body covered in sores. A cold, dry, rigid depression is associated with the image of old Saturn; his chronicity often manifests physically in disease or psychically in a pessimistic rhetoric.

Walter Otto associates Dionysus with moistness.[71] This implies that a Dionysiac depression, being moist, would compensate the dryness and rigidity of a Saturnian depression. It could be called a Dionysiac consciousness that, being close to death, is close to depression; the moistness may be sensed in the tears accompanying an emotion. Greek medicine saw tears in connection with the element of water.[72] Moistness, in relation to emotion, appears also in the alchemical imagination of tears as *aqua lacrimae*. There is a great deal to say about the relationship between Dionysus and depression. Scholars are mostly attracted to the frenzied and mad aspects of the Dionysiac rituals, but my concern is to pay attention to the slow movements and the insights into the body this propitiates. These are also attributes of Dionysus, providing an imagination which brings the psyche closer to depression. It is with this slow motion that Dionysus helps us to accept depression. There is an image of Dionysus facing backward and drinking wine from a *kantaros* while riding a donkey. The donkey is ubiquitous in the Mediterranean scenery. Its slowness provides the right metaphor to match the slowness of depression, and it is a metaphor that propitiates incubation, that realm so basic to the art of psychotherapy. The following, very Dionysiac, imagery of body and death from Niel Micklem is to be read with this slowness of body and soul, bearing in mind Heraclitus's saying that Dionysus and Hades are one and the same:

> Hades introduces the motif of death. No discussion on the body can be sufficient without it. Hades and the body may at first glance seem remote from each other, yet there is indeed an essential relationship and, if confir-

mation is needed, it becomes abundantly clear from two commonplace observations: that Hades is the Greek god of death and that death enters the world with the body and remains its constant companion throughout the span of life.[73]

Before turning to the *Bacchae* of Euripides, it might be good to touch again on the speculations about Dionysus's origins. The scholars have traced his origins to Asia or Thrace, a theory that has caused much controversy; there has also been too much literalization in their studies. In reality, Dionysus was very Greek and appears in the Linear B tablets, which date from around 1250 B.C. and are among the first written Greek records. Euripides describes Dionysus as arriving from abroad, although having a mother who was born in Thebes. For Euripides, therefore, Dionysus is both local and foreign at the same time, and this is often how he appears in dreams: a foreigner who is familiar, a seeming paradox that could make for psychic movement. In ritual, Dionysus is invoked as one who comes from outside: "Come, come, come, Dionysus!" is the sort of invocation that pertains to most Dionysiac religions. He is always a foreigner because of the natural repression pertaining to his archetypal configuration, which makes him appear as if coming from abroad. I believe the reader will not find it difficult to appreciate how, psychologically speaking, that which is closest to us (the body into which we are born) is, at the same time, that which is most foreign to us.

Throughout this essay I have frequently mentioned the body in relation to Dionysus. Here, I would like to repeat that to live in the body is very difficult and alien for us, as alien as the Greeks imagined the origins of Dionysus to be. All too easily any connection to the body is lost. To write about the possible relationship between the psychic body and all that underlies psychosomatics is beyond anyone's possibilities, but we can begin to have an awareness of the psychological body when we become conscious of our alienation from the body, when we become conscious of how easy it is to lose our connection to it. Through this consciousness, if we are patient, we can grow into a relationship with the body and form a possible psychological connection to it.

In modern psychology, as with Dionysus, there is very little discussion about the psychic body and our connection to it. But here, in the context of the body, is the place to discuss Dionysus and the theater. The art of Dionysus par excellence is seen in the theater. We cannot conceive of a good actor who does not have a consciousness of the body. One's thoughts move into the fascinating field of the actor's training, a discipline in which the psychology of the body becomes a painful reality and words and the body of the actor must come together in a Dionysiac consciousness. Such a combination of words and body constellate the Dionysiac strata of the psyche not only in the actor but also in the psychotherapist.

Euripides wrote the *Bacchae* in his old age while he was in voluntary exile in Macedonia, a place where Dionysiac rites certainly retained more archaic traits than in Athens. There, Dionysiac emotions were mostly contained in the theater and its ritual. It was the second part of the above mentioned Orphic myth, the part in which Dionysus is the son of Zeus and Semele, that was the basis of Euripides' conception of the god. The *Bacchae* opens with the entrance of Dionysus. The stage directions describe him as having a crown of ivy, a *thyrsus* in his hand, and a fawn skin draped over his body. He has long flowing hair and a youthful, almost feminine, beauty. One's attention is drawn to his androgyny. Euripides' stage instructions for an androgynous image of Dionysus abound in the complexities of Dionysiac psychology. We have to remember that the actor wore a mask to portray Dionysus's youthful feminine beauty, forcing him to express himself through his body.

Dionysus proceeds to introduce himself:

> I am Dionysus, son of Zeus. My mother was
> Semele, Cadmus' daughter. From her womb the fire
> Of a lightning-flash delivered me. I have come here
> To Thebes and her two rivers, Dirce and Ismenus,
> Veiling my godhead in a mortal shape . . . . (p. 191)

A great deal has been written about this first entrance, referring it to the two levels of the divine and the human in Dionysus's presence and speech. This speech conveys the paradoxical feeling that the actor is Dionysus and he is not Dionysus. In other words, this introduces the secret of Dionysus's psychology, teaching the audience how to be Dionysiac without identifying with the god. Paradox is also the favorite expression of Hermes; it conveys consciousness and unconsciousness at the same time. Of course, Euripides was a man of the theater, and this play is a lesson for actors in how to play a role without identifying with its psychic contents, in this case the role of Dionysus. Throughout the play, Euripides insists on this essential teaching. Later, in the same speech, Dionysus says: "I have changed my form and taken the likeness of a man" (p. 193). It seems to me that this line expresses a very important attitude in Dionysiac psychology. If we identify with the role we are playing in life, then we are already Titanic, for identification is the essence of Titanism. Later in the play, Euripides comes back to the same theme with Dionysus's reply to a question from Pentheus:

Pentheus:
How comes it that you bring these rituals to Hellas?
Dionysus:
Dionysus, son of Zeus, himself instructed me. (p. 206)

These lines have a wider connotation if we do not reduce the Dionysiac ritual to only that of the maenads on the mountain, but see ritual as the essence of the Dionysiac way of life.

With regard to Dionysus's androgynous appearance, Thomas A. Carpenter works out the transition of the bearded Dionysus to the beardless youth portrayed by Euripides. It seems that thereafter the youthful and masked Dionysus dominated the iconography.[74] One feels there must have been a psychological movement throughout the history of tragic poetry up to the appearance of Dionysus in the *Bacchae.* Michael Jameson mentions Aeschylus's reference to the androgynous Dionysus in *Lykurgus,* in which he appears as a secondary figure.[75] But we can assume there was a psychological inner collective process leading to Euripides' conception of the god. He put the god of theater on stage and moreover made him androgynous.

In this culmination of an androgynous Dionysus, one imagines there were historical complexes at work. Euripides must have felt a great collective suffering at the back of his representation of the god. It is something of a challenge to imagine how the Athenian audience reacted to the god of theater as an image of androgyny. Did they feel the usual repugnance provoked by this image? The appearance of the hermaphrodite in dreams is invariably repugnant to the dreamer. Alchemical images of the hermaphrodite are likewise very repulsive and mad, but this repulsive image can also be seen as a Dionysiac ingredient that contains madness.

Euripides' image of Dionysus puts the god at the farthest point from the Greek heroic tradition; this is exemplified by the men who fought in the Trojan War. The *Bacchae* and *Iphigenia in Aulis* were the last two of Euripides' tragedies. His Trojan plays—for which one has to give him credit for showing, for the first time in history, the psychopathic psychology of the heroes—were behind him.[76]

The placing of Dionysus in opposition to the heroic, political, power-ridden psychopath Pentheus seems to be a reflection of what drove Euripides out of Athens and into exile in Macedonia. The way in which he makes Dionysus destroy Pentheus in the *Bacchae* confronts us with two psychological levels for consideration: the inner Dionysiac revenge on a personality that has repressed piety and the Dionysiac way of life, driving it into madness and destruction, and the outer view of Athens taken over by political, psychopathic Titanism at the time of the Peloponnesian War, resulting in the final chapter of great tragic poetry. Euripides was in exile because of the Titanic political power on the loose in his beloved Athens. E. R. Dodds describes the political repression and persecution in Athens at that time:

> But the most striking evidence of the reaction against the Enlightenment is to be seen in the successful prosecutions of intellectuals on religious grounds which took place in Athens in the last third of the fifth century. About 432

B.C. or a year or two later, disbelief in the
supernatural and the teaching of astronomy
were made indictable offences. The next thirty-
odd years witness a series of heresy trials
which is unique in Athenian history. The vic-
tims included most of the leaders of progressive thought at Athens—Anaxagoras, Diagoras, Socrates, almost certainly Protagoras
also, and possibly Euripides. In all these cases
save the last the prosecution was successful:
Anaxagoras may have been fined and ban-
ished; Diagoras escaped by flight; so, probably,
did Protagoras; Socrates, who could have done
the same, or could have asked for a sentence of
banishment, chose to stay and drink the hem-
lock. All these were famous people. How many
obscurer persons may have suffered for their
opinions we do not know. But the evidence we
have is more than enough to prove that the
Great Age of Greek Enlightenment was also,
like our own time, an Age of Persecution—
banishment of scholars, blinkering of thought,
and even (if we can believe the tradition about
Protagoras) burning of books.[77]

Dodds's picture brings home just how much Euripides
must have suffered in Athens before he went into exile.
We can see the psychology of exile in Euripides.

At the beginning, Zeus intended Dionysus to have
dominion over the world, a preference which shows us
the Greek imagination in action.[78] It is a father/son relationship that draws our attention. Apollo was called the
consciousness of Zeus, a father/son relationship in which
the son embodies a new historical and intellectual consciousness that is assimilated by the father. The
father/son relationship of Zeus and Dionysus was very
different: the father accepts the darkness, androgyny,
and drunkenness of his son, who is also the god of the-

ater and tragedy, as well as of women. A psychological view of the myth would see dominion over the world to mean dominion over the psyche, something that gives pause for thought. However, my own view is to conceive of Zeus's intention in regard to Dionysus in terms of the Greek awareness of a personality archetypally ruled by, or centered in, a Dionysiac consciousness and therefore a tragic consciousness. Following this train of thought, we have to see it as a consciousness of a natural conflict, personified by Dionysus and the Titans; it is a tragic consciousness in which a conflicting image balances the personality, or in which Dionysus is assimilated together with his archetypal complexities. In any event, it is a very complex image that is part of our being.

We also have to appreciate that, for the Greeks, Dionysus with his tragic conflict was the fulfillment of the Greek culture: "It was Zeus who brought fulfillment, but it was Dionysus who completed the fulfillment—or to use a modern expression, 'set the crown on the world's creation,'"[79] a projection that could be a metaphor for the possibility of psychic balance in a world that is obviously ruled by the Titans. Another aspect of this father/son relationship is that of Zeus as the image-maker and Dionysus, his son, as the incarnation of the image of androgyny in the body. Taking these aspects of Dionysus's psychology further reminds us again of the tradition that equated Dionysus and Ariadne with Eros and Psyche and thus to conceive that the androgynous Dionysus contains within himself the dynamism of Eros and Psyche.

Dionysus's androgyny moves us into depth psychology. Jung worked extensively on androgyny and gave great importance to it. He made a strong equation between the Self, that which regulates the balance of the personality, and the hermaphrodite, that which synthesizes the union of the male/female opposition. This

allows us to speculate that the Dionysus portrayed by
Euripides was a personification of the Self. We have to
remember that the Rebis, as the hermaphrodite, was the
final product of the alchemical process. It may be a bold
association to conceive the appearance of the androgynous Dionysus in tragedy as the result of a similar
process.

In *Hermes and His Children,* I discuss the hermaphrodite as a product of the psychological tension created
by longing and rejection, and how the dynamism of this
tension brings about the conjunction of the opposites,
expressed in the union of male and female in the image
of the hermaphrodite.[80] It is possible to imagine that a
similar process went on among the Greek tragic poets
until Euripides' androgynous Dionysus arrived on the
scene. In the same work, I also refer to the "weakness"
of the hermaphrodite, which I see as an important
aspect of Dionysiac consciousness. Any approach to
Dionysus should include this "weakness." It would be
farcical to approach this god within the framework of a
high-flying ego. This weakness plays an important part
in the formation of a psychotherapist. The therapist
with a strong ego polarizes the unconscious.

Dionysus's first entrance can be likened to an image
in a dream; in order to approach such an image, consciousness has to be at a symmetrical level with that
image, a level I associate with the alchemical *media
natura,* a consciousness that exemplifies the Dionysiac
demands of the theater and a Dionysiac vision of life.
Dreams in which theater appears have the connotation
of a possible beginning of a Dionysiac consciousness and
reflection. For instance, I cannot imagine Shakespeare's
"all the world's a stage" or Calderon's *El gran teatro del
mundo* without this consciousness and a Dionysiac
worldview.

Dionysus comes onstage full of jealousy and revenge. He has come to take revenge upon his mother's sisters because of their negation of his godhead. He goes on to tell us that he has driven his mother's sisters mad because, owing to their envy, they twisted the reality of his birth by saying that he was not the son of Zeus. Envy is an emotion, so from the beginning we are in the realm of emotions and madness.

In the play, Semele has three sisters, Agauë, Autonoë, and Ino. Including Semele, this makes four sisters in all. This is a familiar motif in fairy-tale literature, where envy is likely to appear. The paradigm for the fairy tale is the myth of Eros and Psyche. One of Psyche's first tasks was to get rid of her three envious sisters. Euripides' genius brought this motif into tragedy, into the exact opposite of fairy-tale psychology. Instead of getting rid of the sisters magically, he had Dionysus drive them mad, a tragic madness:

> Therefore I have driven those same sisters mad, turned them
> All frantic out of doors, their home now is the mountain;
> Their wits are gone. I have made them bear the emblem of
> My mysteries. . . . (p. 192)

In his book *Envy and the Greeks*, Peter Walcot shows the importance of envy among the Greeks. For example, envy was the concern of communal life: the Greek who created communal envy knew that he would have to pay for this with ostracism.[81] Walcot notes how, above all, it appeared in the most closely related people: in family members and friends. He paints an excellent picture of envy in pagan times, before Christianity had made it a capital sin and by so doing repressed awareness of it. More importantly, Walcot makes one think about how to differentiate envy and jealousy, the two emotions that often overlap and create confusion in Western culture.[82]

Envy is a more common emotion than we tend to think. And when we are taken over by envy, it blinds us where emotions are concerned. For me, the common envy of someone's fortune is a secondary issue. I am interested in tracking down the madness that springs forth when one compares oneself to someone else and in so doing is alienated from oneself.

Just as envy appears in the tale of Eros and Psyche or the *Bacchae,* so it appears in psychotherapy, sometimes revealing itself as an aspect of the personality, sometimes as the dominant component of a psychosis, and sometimes as a psychosomatic ailment. Envy arises when a personality is unable to accept its selfhood or its limitations. Envy can become a split-off complex acting autonomously, making any reflection difficult if not impossible. In order for the psychotherapist to detect the appearance of envy in the psyche he or she has to be acquainted with this emotion. Luck also is needed, as envy is so often hidden. However, in Euripides' tragedy, it is transparently clear that Agauë, Ino, and Autonoë are possessed with the madness of Dionysus because of their envy of Semele, his mother.

In three sentences that make an image, Dionysus introduces the main mortal protagonist of the tragedy—Pentheus, the son of the eldest sister, Agauë:

Now Cadmus has made over his throne and kingly
 honours
To Pentheus, son of his eldest daughter Agauë. He
Is a fighter against gods, defies me, excludes me from
Libations, never names me in prayers. Therefore I will
Demonstrate to him, and to all Thebes, that I am a god.
(p. 193)

In these lines, Dionysus, onstage and full of emotion, expresses very clearly his jealousy—the old jealousy of the gods. As with envy, the jealousy of the gods is waiting for some differentiation. Mythologically speaking, one can imagine that each god or goddess shows his or her jealousy in different ways. We can also see that, in this part of Dionysus's speech, what he says about Pentheus refers, in the language of Jung's psychology, to his unlived complexes in relation to Dionysus: those complexes that he has repressed and so not experienced.

In the great literary tradition of Western culture, Shakespeare expresses Othello's jealousy as sexual; it becomes a state of possession, leading to tragic destruction. Jealousy as so expressed by Shakespeare is direct and sexually motivated and quite different from Euripides' vision of a god's jealousy. In the tale, *La Gitanilla,* Cervantes writes about jealousy, but in contrast to Shakespeare's Othello, his Gitanilla is described as wise because she knows about jealousy, knows about a shadow out of which great knowledge can come. Jealousy can overtake any one of us in a given moment. A god's jealousy, on the other hand, is provoked when the god is rejected or not recognized in the archetypal way of life represented by the deity, such as Euripides depicts in relation to Dionysus.

Although the attitudes of these two great writers toward jealousy are classic, that of Euripides merits more attention from students of psychology in that it offers the possibility to understand just what the repression of a god like Dionysus, with all the archetypal complexities he carries, means psychodynamically. The emotion of jealousy appears in psychotherapy, ranging from denying it to being possessed by it. While it is the most human of emotions, it connects us with the animal realm of the instincts. There are cases of jealousy that end in total destruction. The crime reports in the newspapers abound in them. There are marriages dominated by jealousy. In my personal experience, I have known of a woman who was so possessed by jealousy that she felt a great relief when her husband died and of a marriage of twenty-eight years in which the core of the relationship was an obsessive jealousy. I wonder if such a jealousy is merely the cover for, or the container of, a much worse madness?

Euripides' genius was at its peak when he displayed the jealousy of the gods. In *Hippolytus,* he shows how Aphrodite takes her revenge on Hippolytus for not worshipping her divinity. The picture he paints of Phaedra's Aphroditic state of possession, with its whole gamut of symptoms, is impeccable; it is her possession that triggers the plot of the tragedy. In the *Bacchae,* he shows Dionysus taking his revenge on Pentheus for not worshipping him. Both plays give a lesson in the repression that brought about the gods' jealousy: in the case of Hippolytus, it is his rigidity in only worshipping Artemis and thus repressing Aphrodite and her carnality, while in the case of Pentheus, it is his brutal repression of Dionysus.

Dionysus exits, and the chorus enters, composed of *bacchae* or maenads, women whose way of life is centered on and made meaningful through the cult of Dionysus. With regard to the maenads, Kerényi writes:

> Whoever observed them from afar saw them in the various, scarcely distinguishable forms of "the rage": this is perhaps the best translation of our word *mania,* but it must be taken as bearing all its various senses at once—that of

raging love as well as that of raging anger.
This is why the women about Dionysos were
called *mainades,* "Maenads," and the god himself was called *mainomenos* or *mainoles,*
meaning "raging" in this extended sense of the
word.[83]

We should start to make a differentiation between
the maenads' ritualistic madness, which the god both
causes and "cures," and the madness of the jealous god's
revenge, in which he drives the possessed to destruction.
The play shows both of these sorts of madness. To keep
their difference in mind is very important, because it is
basic to our understanding of Dionysiac psychology.

The maenads come onstage dancing, moving to the
rhythm of flutes and drums. They, too, are crowned with
wreaths of ivy, wear white tunics, and carry *thyrsuses.* I
imagine that they come onstage dancing softly, moving
their bodies slowly.

In the first strophe, the chorus sings that they come
from afar, from the holy mountain:

We run with the god of laughter;
Labour is joy and weariness is sweet,
And our song resounds to Bacchus! (p. 193)

Evidently, they do not feel tired. Dancing without
fatigue is a motif that appeared too in the dream of the
Venezuelan woman. The line "Labour is joy and weariness is sweet" conveys to us the psychic achievement of
Dionysiac women and belongs to their soul's alchemy.
This is a paradox similar to "a sweet suffering, a soft
wound," as the final goal of Sir George Ripley's alchemical opus. Alchemy can help us to read the image in
depth. I try to assimilate "sweet suffering" to a consciousness that is somehow able to integrate and trans-
form suffering into an experience of the soul. The image

of the maenads reveals more about Dionysiac psychology than any speculation we can bring to it. But to come back to the Titans for a moment: "sweet suffering" is in contrast to Titanic suffering, which is empty, existential, repetitive, and without any possibility of reflection and consciousness.

Here one sees joy, a very strong and unique feeling, as an attribute of Dionysus. It is an emotion that accompanies many other sorts of feelings, as Euripides' lines exemplify.

The chorus continues in the second strophe:

Blest is the happy man
Who knows the mysteries the gods ordain,
And sanctifies his life,
Joins soul with soul in mystic unity,
And, by due ritual made pure,
Enters the ecstasy of mountain solitudes . . . . (p. 194)

From these lines we can assume that Euripides knew about the mystic experience of Dionysus. I consider this a very important strophe, because it shows solitude not only as an individual experience but also something that can happen within a group. "Mystic unity" and "ritual made pure" perhaps indicates a mysticism that does not need any forced ascesis.

Then, in a very moving scene, Tiresias, an old seer, enters and, although blind, makes his way to the door of Pentheus's palace and knocks. He is looking for his old friend Cadmus and calls for him, saying:

. . . I'm an old man, and he's older still—
But we agreed to equip ourselves with Bacchic wands
And fawnskin cloaks, and put on wreaths of ivy-shoots.
    (p. 197)

The two old friends are dressing themselves for an orgy. Tiresias personifies inner wisdom and divination, while Cadmus, the father of Semele (mother of Dionysus), personifies tradition. Together they plan to celebrate Dionysus in the mountains. These two old men represent the psychology of an old age that surrenders itself to Dionysus, and it is my great interest to approach old age from within the archetypal realm of Dionysus. Cadmus says: "I could drum the ground all night / And all day too, without being tired" (p. 197). Their decision to go to the mountain on foot demonstrates Dionysiac energy in old age. Cadmus's words are an image of what the Dionysiac dance is all about, a dance in which any rigidity in the old man's body falls away. Dance is not only one of the oldest expressions of humankind, animals also dance. In dreams, dancing conveys that the dreamer is connecting to a very archaic, instinctive, emotional expression of the body; it can be taken as an internal Dionysiac imagery of the soul and the body. In any given moment, we can be accompanied by an inner image of dancing. In my commentary on García Lorca's *Theory and Play of the Duende,* I mention an old lady who won the prize in a flamenco competition simply by standing up and turning her body.[84] In the very Dionysiac art of flamenco, old age signifies knowledge and ripeness. When old people sing and dance flamenco, they are intensely moving, because they are dancing as old people. The Dionysiac dance has an ageless quality and can be danced by all ages, from a tiny child to an old person. There is no ideal age for a Dionysiac way of life. Flamenco dancing really stirs the imagination, and it gives us a notion of what the maenads' dance might have been like in ancient times.

We live in a world in which the dominant model for life is that of youth. Thus we see today old people in the sad condition of being unable to live in the here and now of old age, people in their seventies still clinging pathetically to a youthful way of life, seemingly unaware of the years to come. As far as I know, modern psychology has not discussed or explored the possibilities of Dionysus in old age. In Jungian psychology, for example, old age is reflected in the two-headed archetype of the puer and the senex, the archetype that fundamentally rules consciousness throughout a lifetime, a register of the almanac in both chronological and psychological terms, so to say.

The great pioneers of modern psychology have written very little about their own psyches in old age. Under the circumstances, it is understandable that psychologists tend to follow the collective trend of repressing anything that might have to do with a psychology of old age. However, I find it difficult to accept that there are those in their eighties who continue to discuss vehemently their theories about childhood and yet offer no testimony to the emotional life of their old age. The fact of the matter is that the overwhelming dramatic force of old age makes its psychology a very difficult task, one that is very far from the realm of easy words. The emotions engendered by images remain as inner experiences, soul experiences, giving rise to desperation when faced with the inability to express them in words.

We have to appreciate that our current approach to old age is very rational and one-sided, dominated by the up-to-date conception of providing quality of life through a barrage of remedies. Thus the aged are circumscribed within modern medicine's trend of "normal" speech and behavior, and the emotional life, the memories, and the soul are excluded. The insistence on an idealized image of youth only exacerbates anxiety in old age, blocking an acceptance of the slow depression needed at that time of life. For it is in old age that the body becomes an unparalleled living experience and takes on an almost overwhelming reality, its presence constantly felt, sometimes like a trap. It is in old age that the body wields its authority and there arises another consciousness of the body. We know very little about the psychology of the body, but Dionysus could be taken as a metaphorical vehicle to connect to it. The physical limitations of old age provide a propitious field for insight into the psychic emotional body. It is a time when Dionysus is present more frequently than we think, present in the body and in the emotions that arise in the face of illness and death. Old age demands a tragic consciousness.

There is not much discussion about the suffering of the psyche in old age, the way in which the natural forces of anxiety and depression, which have accompanied one throughout one's life, now take on a new status and demand a new initiation and understanding. It is during these years that anxiety appears in different and bizarre guises. We can imagine the anxiety engendered in trying unsuccessfully to remember the name of someone met only fleetingly or only heard about. It is, however, through such a guise that the unequivocal emotion of anxiety can be detected as being present. For me, the importance lies not in the loss of memory itself but in the accompanying anxiety that was hidden. The image is intact, but access to it is lost. Here one sees that it is more therapeutic to accept the reality of the anxiety, which can move the psyche, than to fall into the trap of trying to "heal" the lost memory. Not only names, but the loss of memory of events, events with no visual image associated with them, also create confusion and anxiety. I believe these tricks of the memory, something which is so close to the soul, are not appreciated enough.[85]

The force of depression is felt, painfully, in the suddenly diminishing physical activity, the slower movements and loss of flexibility. We are forced to realize also that the illnesses, suffered through the years, now have to be carried and contained by a physical body in decline, and this new reality feeds the depression. A possible response to this challenge would be for a Dionysiac "psychological body" to take over and compensate this new reality, thus giving a more adequate approach to the depression. In other words, life demands a more psychic response to the challenge of the physical body in decline. It might be that the awareness of how these two opposites, anxiety and depression, make their presence felt at this time of life could be the basis for initiation into old age.

One of my intentions is to look behind distorted images of Dionysus, such as the drinking and sexual "jolly Bacchus" mentioned in Dodds's passage, and to rescue those elements that I consider precious for depth psychology. T. S. Eliot's line, "Old men ought to be explorers," should be read with the Dionysiac psychology of old age in mind.[86] It is the repression of the image of old age that makes life so difficult for the old person at a time when new limitations and afflictions have to be accepted, when a true Dionysiac imagery is most needed. In other words, the psychological reality of having repressed for a lifetime that which could now bring some fulfillment. Fulfillment in old age is to be found in simple things: the shedding of two tears at the theater; the emotion felt in Dionysiac music; conversation with a friend over a bottle of wine; the appearance, after a night full of anxiety and depression, of a soul image, which shakes the body with emotion and gives feeling to the solitude of old age. The psyche sustains and nourishes itself with emotions arising from within and without. They are not difficult to recognize as Dionysiac, because they are accompanied by tragic or aesthetic images.

At this time of life, emotions are felt as a source of life, felt as never before with a consciousness nearer to the unknown sources from which dreams arise. We know that the dream is at the core of primitive man's survival and is the foundation of religion; it also assures our psychic health. This consciousness in old age, nearer to the unknown part of human nature, has been seen traditionally and historically in the guise of the old wise man or the old fool. We have also to see that this dreamlike consciousness, or *media natura* consciousness, in being Dionysiac can be confusing and quite removed from the certainties of modern approaches to geriatric psychology.

My contention is to value the authority of the body in old age, to make it central to the psyche's complexities. I would go so far as to say that old age is the "golden" age for Dionysus: the time for being alone in the body, alone with Dionysus. It is this reality that has led me to conceive of old age as being centered in the body. Let me illustrate this through the two aspects of the verb "to be" in the Spanish language: *ser* and *estar*. *Ser* relates to the permanent condition of "being," whereas *estar* relates to the circumstance of "being." To live one's old age as I have described above gives priority to the state of *estar*, that is to say, in the here and now, to stay in the body and feel it. All the philosophical speculations, all the psychological theories one has learned, founded on the *ser* aspect of the verb—all those questions and speculations about "being"—have had to submit to *estar*. However, to live in the *estar* is not so easy, for it is complex and not always comfortable. It belongs to the most subjective aspect of the psyche and a Dionysiac consciousness in old age. To understand one's madness differs at each stage of life, and old age demands a deeper acquaintance with madness, and this is in itself a Dionysiac proposition.

Pentheus now makes his first appearance onstage, accompanied by his guards. He gives the impression of a tyrant who rules with a military hand and has pronounced Titanic traits, as will become apparent. I see Pentheus as a personification of those power-ridden, political, Athenian Titans who drove Euripides into exile. A combination of Titanism and tyranny leads to the repression of the Dionysiac way of life. Pentheus has just heard that the women of Thebes, including his mother and aunts, are dancing to Dionysus in the mountains. His first words are, "They are Maenad priestesses, if you please! / Aphrodite supplants Bacchus in their ritual" (p. 198). Such confusion merits discussion, for Pentheus can neither respect nor differentiate Dionysiac characteristics and falls into the typical confusion of mixing the archetypes.

Pentheus represents the Titanic part of human nature in opposition to Dionysus, the forces of power and of a repressive establishment. When he hears about the maenads in the mountains, he confuses the Dionysiac cult with that of Aphrodite, a goddess to whom divine madness was also attributed. We have to credit Euripides for his presentation twenty-five centuries ago of this confusion that has been repeated again and again throughout history.

In the nineteenth century, at the end of the Victorian era when the pioneers of modern psychology were exploring neurosis and psychosis, it occurred to them to attribute the cause to sexuality. We can now conjecture that psychology's fuss about, and fixation on, sexuality is an unconscious way of repressing Dionysus. Here, Euripides can help us again: his portrayal of Phaedra's possession by Aphrodite's sexuality shows her to be suffering a complex psychosomatic condition created by the conflict between her possession induced by Aphrodite and her moralistic complexes—the *aidos* of Phaedra.[87] Although the picture it brings is tragic, it is also "civilized"; it happens in Troezen, near Athens, whereas the Dionysiac possession of Agaüe is, by comparison, uniquely archaic and happens in the mountains near Thebes. Agaüe's possession would seem to come about through the conflict of two forces in opposition—Dionysus and the Titans. The image of Agaüe's possession connects us to unconscious and very complex levels of human nature. The Dionysiac and the Aphroditic archetypal realms call for differentiation, although Euripides shows that they can also be brought together when, with its second entrance, the chorus of maenads sings in praise of Aphrodite, a song which comes out of their Dionysiac bodies and emotions:

O to set foot on Aphrodite's island,
On Cyprus,
Take me, O Bromius, take me and inspire
Laughter and worship! There our holy spell
And ecstasy are welcome; there the gentle band
Of Graces have their home, and sweet Desire. (p. 204)

Here, through the song of the maenads, Euripides describes a quality of Aphrodite's sexuality to be understood as a sexuality lived and enjoyed in a Dionysiac body, a sexuality experienced as a sacrament. The words *holy spell* and *ecstasy* evoke an image of a sexuality akin to the mystical experience attributed to Dionysus that we discussed earlier. The chorus sings to the communion of two deities—Dionysus, under his surname of Bromios, and Aphrodite, the lady from Cyprus. Such a communion brings a short-lived, mystical sexual blessing; it brings a momentary spark. This imagery of the *Bacchae* throws some light onto the confusion concerning sexuality, a confusion that evidently existed in pagan times and, as we have seen, pertains to the repression of Dionysus. I think we cannot go wrong by saying that, in modern psychology, sexuality has been discussed with a Titanic ego, which leads us even further away from Euripides' image: the maenad who longed for sexuality and experienced it in her Dionysiac body.

The communion of Aphrodite and Dionysus in relation to sexuality can be seen as a way into a Dionysiac consciousness. Sexuality in itself without the body of Dionysus, becomes merely a childish hysterical frustration. Another possibility in this communion would be to see sexuality as an initiation into Dionysiac madness; in other words, to accept sexuality as an imaginative erotic vehicle for connecting to Dionysiac madness. This is an adult view very unlike the schemes of modern psychiatry and psychotherapy. Aphrodite and Dionysus become the archetypal frame for the functioning of this instinct with its wide possibilities and its strong presence in psyche.

Pentheus vows to destroy Dionysus. Then he notices Tiresias and Cadmus and shouts at them mockingly:

Why look! Another miracle! Here's Teiresias
The prophet—in a fawnskin; and my mother's father—
A Bacchant with a fennel-wand! Well, there's a sight
For laughter!

He continues to insult the two old men, and Tiresias replies:

. . . Your fluent tongue
Promises wisdom; but the content of your speech
Is ignorant. Power and eloquence in a headstrong man
Spell folly; such a man is a peril to the state.
(pp. 199–200)

These lines reinforce my idea that Pentheus can be taken as a model for an Athenian politician.

Tiresias tries unsuccessfully to get Pentheus to give up his idea of destroying Dionysus, and in a long speech intended to soothe Pentheus's mind, he touches at the source of Western culture:

> In human affairs: first, Demeter—the same goddess
> Is also Earth; give her which name you please—and she
> Supplies mankind with solid food. After her came
> Dionysos, Semele's son; the blessing he procured
> And gave to men is counterpart to that of bread:
> The clear juice of the grape. When mortals drink
>   their fill
> Of wine, the sufferings of our unhappy race
> Are banished, each day's troubles are forgotten in sleep.
> There is no other cure for sorrow. (p. 200)

Tiresias expresses the down-to-earth truth of the bread and wine, attributed respectively to Demeter and Dionysus. It is a truth of such magnitude that Christianity has used the bread and wine to express the mystery of the Eucharist. At another level, bearing in mind the innate ambivalence in relation to Dionysus, we note that what for Tiresias is a blessing, for someone else could be a curse. With that, we are into the madness of addiction. One of Dionysus's names is Oinos, "wine." Wine itself is the name of a god, and there is no doubt that to drink a glass of wine gives the most immediate access to Dionysus in the body.

The above lines should be considered within a geographical and racial context: bread from wheat and wine from grapes were originally Mediterranean cultural achievements. Hesiod repeatedly warned against people who did not eat bread, that is, barbarians.[88] I prefer to see Dionysus as the god of drunkenness and intoxication (states that occur in all cultures) within this geographical context, leaving out any connection he might have to similar divinities in other religions.

In two works, *Greek Piety* and *Greek Folk Religion,* Nilsson draws attention to the importance of libation in daily family life, symposium, and religious rituals.[89] In the household, the day began with a libation to Hestia, the goddess of the hearth, or to *Agathos Daimon,* and throughout the day there were libations to other deities. It is noteworthy that through the wine of Dionysus, in a highly individual religious ritual, the connection was made to other gods and goddesses, that is to say, to different forms and ways of life. Euripides, in the first speech of the *Bacchae,* shows that one of the things angering Dionysus was that Pentheus excluded him from libations.

When Tiresias says, "The suffering of our unhappy race," he is probably referring to Titanic suffering. I see Dionysiac culture as compensating daily, repetitive Titanic suffering with wine. Euripides' poetic lines and Nilsson's scholarship on libation express the Dionysiac roots of the Mediterranean peoples' culture.

In his book *Dionysos,* Kerényi has worked on the tales of the origin of wine and the drinking of wine within the myth of Dionysus's arrival:

> Ikarios was bestowing the gift of wine. In an ox cart he was carrying full wineskins about through the mountainous regions of Attica, then inhabited by wild shepherds. The shepherds became drunk, thought they were poisoned . . . and murdered Ikarios . . . .
>
> There is nothing improbable about the assumption that the wine introduced from outside underwent a split into two persons, god and hero, Dionysos and Ikarios.[90]

We need not leave this tale behind in classical times. It is very alive, evidenced by such excessive drinking as goes on in our times. During my childhood, I heard tales of drinking and dancing parties among the peasants that ended in the wielding of machetes and death. In another guise, it is the mayhem and carnage in a tavern at the end of a western (that is, the film genre). These are examples of the extreme and tragic appearances of Dionysus; more common and universal is an initiation into drinking. The tales of Icarius might have the didactic purpose of both a warning and an initiation (with respect to the latter, in how to drink wine with the addition of water). Most of us can remember a milder initiation, generally in adolescence, when we did not know how to drink and ended up with a heavy hangover, and also how long it took us to learn to drink properly, in what might be called a civilized manner, and so avoid the danger of drunken madness.

Erwin Rohde, in *Psyche,* makes the connection of Dionysus to the ritualistic use of cannabis.[91] It is a mild drug and has been used in the initiatory rites of the autochthonous peoples of Central America. During the 1960s, we heard many stories of the emotions that accompany the smoking of "pot," including the so-called bad trip, in which Dionysus brings a sort of paranoiac madness. While cannabis gives pleasure to the senses of some users, Dionysus makes his true epiphany in the bad trip, in which there is an experience of madness. Here we can differentiate two aspects of Dionysus: procuring stimulus for the senses and inducing transitional madness that can teach the psyche. The bad trip, with its negative paranoiac fantasies and feelings, can be more profitable for the maturing of the personality than the good trip with its pleasure to the senses and ecstasy.

Kerényi, in *Dionysos,* works out the relation between Dionysus and the poppy seed, seeing the smoking of opium, a very addictive drug, as a Cretan conception which sought a mystical experience, but one to be distinguished from the "pure" mystical experience sung to by the chorus. We cannot escape the fact that Dionysus would seem to be the god of strong addictions, whether it be of alcohol or opiates. Basically, addiction involves a craving for wine, strong spirits, or drugs, and it is notable that alcoholics and drug addicts do not eat, as if the connection between Demeter and Dionysus were broken. In Euripides' strophe, wine and bread are brought together, as if to complement each other. The two deities together make for an archetypal structure of culture—bread and wine. Here, we can begin to reflect upon the psychology of those people who do not succeed in going through the Dionysiac initiation of wine and drugs and so remain caught in the madness of addiction.

Rather than considering here how modern psychiatry has dealt with addiction, I propose that the psychology of addiction be completely assumed into the archetypal realm of Dionysus, the god of wine and opiates, because then it can be perceived as having a tragic component. Addiction is, in reality, the tragedy of a person bent on pursuing his or her own destruction: it is a tragic condition, rather than a vice, as traditionally viewed, or a disease, as it is from contemporary medical or psychiatric standpoints.

The beneficial effects of wine drinking have recently become part of the medical and scientific media's obsession with cholesterol rather than the continuation of an ancient cultural tradition that enriches life. With a bit of imagination, we can see that this rhetoric participates in the ongoing battle between Dionysus and the Titans: the dangerous acceleration of today's Titanic mentality is reduced by taking a glass or two of wine at lunch. I see this as the taming of the Titans' accelerated impulses. Even more recently, however, there came a report that the skins of the grapes prevent infarcts and cancer. The medical profession, in its anxiety to prevent alcoholism and addiction, is bent on producing a pill with the same properties as the grape skins. Dionysus's culture of the wine is repressed yet again. Titanic science lacks the imagination to appreciate that a glass of good red wine speaks to the heart in more ways than one and can only heal it.

Here, it is perhaps relevant to recall a very special, historical, collective repression of Dionysus, in this case, the culture of wine. In the middle of the nineteenth century, a group of American politicians visited the wine regions of France. Coming from a money-oriented and progressive society, they were struck by the backwardness and poverty in the region and unable to see the culture in the life of the people there. Upon their return to the United States, they passed a law prohibiting the production of wine, being convinced that wine and poverty went hand in hand and missing altogether the connection between wine and culture. Later, in the early part of the twentieth century, after the passing of the notorious Prohibition laws with their brutal consequences, Dionysus took his revenge in bootlegging, gangsters, and violence. Even now, at the end of the century, and even though the United States is now a wine-producing country, these past repressions of a Dionysiac wine culture have left scars on the American society. Furthermore, because of continued repression, they seem impossible to heal; the United States, in spite of its so-called war on drugs, is the greatest consumer of addictive substances in the world.

After Pentheus exits, Tiresias makes a precise diagnosis of Pentheus's state of mind:

> Foolhardy man! You do not know what you have said.
> Before, you were unbalanced; now you are insane.
>   (p. 203)

The two old men set off to "pay due service to Dionysus, son of Zeus." Before they leave, Tiresias makes a sort of prayer:

> Cadmus, the name
> *Pentheus* means *sorrow*. God grant he may not bring
>   sorrow
> Upon your house. Do not take that as prophecy;
> I judge his acts. Such foolish words bespeak a fool.
>   (p. 203)

In this intervention of Tiresias, we find a prognosis by way of prophecy. But we have to realize that this prognostic prophecy is through an understanding of Pentheus's behavior and speech, that is to say, his whole rhetoric. It is the sort of prognosis that is the standard work in modern psychotherapy.

Tiresias and Cadmus leave for the mountain and the chorus responds to Pentheus's tirade against Dionysus:

> Do you hear his blasphemy?
> Pentheus dares—do you hear?—to revile the god of joy,
> The son of Semele, who when the gay-crowned feast is
>   set

Is named among gods the chief;
Whose gifts are joy and union of soul in dancing. (p. 204)

Here again, we see that important gift of Dionysus—joy while dancing, joy as an experience of the soul.

The "union of the soul in dancing" is at the core of the mystical experience in all the Dionysiac religions. From anthropological sources and the history of religion, Dodds gives ample examples of this "union," including this quote from Aldous Huxley in respect to the people of many societies for whom "ritual dances provide a religious experience that seems more satisfying and convincing than any other . . . . It is with their muscles that they most easily obtain knowledge of the divine."[92]

Now we come to the final part of the *Bacchae*. The guards who were sent to arrest Dionysus enter with their prisoner. At the same time, Pentheus enters from the palace. He begins to interrogate Dionysus, in the manner of a chief of security interrogating a terrorist; afterward he sends Dionysus to prison in the stables.

Then Dionysus's voice is heard offstage, calling to his maenads:

Io, Io! Do you know my voice, do you hear?
Worshippers of Bacchus! Io, Io! (p. 210)

But a miracle happens: an earthquake destroys Pentheus's palace and Dionysus is free. He enters again and tells the chorus how he outwitted Pentheus and escaped his bonds. He describes Pentheus's state of mind when Pentheus tried to bind him in the stables:

Then I made a mockery of him. He thought he was
    binding me;
But he neither held nor touched me, save in his deluded
    mind.

> Near the mangers where he meant to tie me up, he
>   found a bull;
> And he tied his rope round the bull's knees and hooves,
>   panting with rage,
> Dripping sweat, biting his lips; while I sat quietly by and
>   watched. (p. 212)

Ruth Padel writes:

> Madness has a nonhuman cause, and nonhu-
> man effects. Both the maddening daemon and
> the maddened person are nonhuman.
> Daemonic causes of madness may be part ani-
> mal. And, like Dionysus, mad. So is their vic-
> tim. When you go mad, you are (like) animal.[93]

Euripides' lines show clearly the meeting between the
mocking daemon that induces madness and Pentheus,
the maddened person who, in his delusion, confuses
Dionysus with a bull. Pentheus is "sick from *phantas-
mata* [appearances, visions]."[94] The bull is closely related to Dionysus and brings to mind the Dionysiac art of
bullfighting: the killing of the bull as a religious enact-
ment of the nonhuman. We can begin to see bullfighting
as a meeting of art and the nonhuman.

Next, Dionysus tells how he produced a phantom
that Pentheus stabbed at, thinking it was Dionysus, and
then Dionysus destroyed the stables, leaving Pentheus
grieved and dazed.

Pentheus comes back onstage and upon seeing
Dionysus, gives an excited shout. A herdsman enters and
reports on the goings-on in the mountains:

> And they [maenads] wore wreaths of ivy-leaves, or oak,
>   or flowers
> Of bryony. One would strike her thyrsus on a rock

And from the rock a limpid stream of water sprang.
Another dug her wand into the earth, and there
The god sent up a fountain of wine. Those who desired
Milk had only to scratch the earth with finger-tips,
And there was the white stream flowing for them to
    drink,
While from the thyrsus a sweet ooze of honey dripped.
    (p. 216)

This is an imaginative evocation of the joie de vivre of
the Dionysiac rituals in the mountains, an image which
has inspired many artists and which might be a component of the fantasy of the jolly Bacchus. But just after
this Arcadian picture, the herdsman describes the other
side of the coin:

Bulls, which one moment felt proud rage hot in their
    horns
The next were thrown bodily to the ground, dragged
    down
By hands of girls in thousands; and they stripped the
    flesh
From the bodies faster than you could wink your royal
    eyes. (p. 217)

This is a horrific picture of the Dionysiac rites at
their most archaic, and it seems to belong to the ritualistic killing of the god as a bull, although in saying this
we fall short of what the image conveys. We cannot really read it.

After listening to the herdsman, Pentheus wants to
mount a military operation and round up the women on
the mountain. He shouts his orders to the guards. But
Dionysus warns him:

... do not take up arms
Against a god. Dionysus will not tolerate
Attempts to drive his worshippers from their holy hills.
(p. 219)

However, Pentheus does not heed him, and it is now that
Dionysus leads him, step by step, into madness.
Dionysus persuades Pentheus to put on women's clothes
and a fawnskin and to hold a thyrsus in his hand so that
he might go to the mountains and spy on the maenads.
Pentheus goes off to change his dress, whereupon
Dionysus says to the chorus:

Women, this man is walking into the net. He will
Visit the Bacchae; and there death shall punish him.
(p. 222)

Dionysus follows Pentheus into the palace to dress him
as a woman for his trip to the mountain. He returns and
calls to Pentheus:

Come, perverse man, greedy for sights you should not
see,
Eager for deeds you should not do—Pentheus! Come out
Before the palace and show yourself to me, wearing
The garb of a frenzied Bacchic woman, and prepared
To spy on your mother and all her Bacchic company.
(p. 224)

Here we have another image of Dionysiac madness.
Dionysus is the only god that dresses as a woman.[95]
Pentheus, who found Dionysus's androgyny so repugnant, is now himself a transvestite. The previous scene,
when Dionysus is persuading Pentheus to dress as a
maenad, can be taken as a metaphor for a man's uncon-

scious need to dress as a woman, a form of Dionysiac madness, or a peculiar way to connect to the god. The somewhat innocuous madness of transvestism is probably holding a madness that otherwise could be very destructive. In our own times, transvestism has manifested in a more or less collective way, although there are individual men who practice it privately, finding in it an intimate feeling of being connected emotionally to something unknown. Dionysus explains his cunning purpose: "to humble him [Pentheus] / From the arrogance he showed when first he threatened me" (p. 222). In other words, to humble the macho Pentheus through transvestism.

Now comes another dialogue that furthers Pentheus's madness. Pentheus says to Dionysus:

You are a bull I see leading me forward now;
A pair of horns seems to have grown upon your head.
Were you a beast before? You have become a bull. (p. 225)

Pentheus sees Dionysus as a bull, the animal in the godhead. Ruth Padel writes, "Inverted vision is central to tragic ideas of madness," and she continues:

Its prime example is the inversion of animal and human. Madness muddles civilization's basic knowledge of what is animal, and what human. Ajax sees animals as men. Other mad figures see people as animals. The invasion of human by animal is implicated in the damage madness does, not only to human form, but to human ways of seeing and understanding.[96]

Dionysus replies to Pentheus:

The god then did not favour us; he is with us now,
We have made our peace with him; you see as you should
see. (p. 225)

That Pentheus confuses the god with a bull makes an extraordinary image of his madness. He is now completely passive ("We have made our peace with him") and asks Dionysus for advice about how he should behave on the mountain.

Now comes a fascinating dialogue between Dionysus and Pentheus, in which the latter sounds rather like a drag queen before a stage performance.

Pentheus:
How do I look? Tell me, is not the way I stand
Like the way Ino stands, or like my mother Agauë?
Dionysus:
Looking at you, I think I see them both. Wait now;
Here is a curl has slipped out of its proper place,
Not as I tucked it carefully below your snood.
Pentheus:
Indoors, as I was tossing my head up and down
Like a Bacchic dancer, I dislodged it from its place.
Dionysus:
Come, then; I am the one who should look after you.
I'll fix it in its place again. There; lift up your head.
Pentheus:
You dress me, please; I have put myself in your hands
    now.
Dionysus:
Your girdle has come loose; and now your dress does not
Hang as it should, in even pleats down to the ankle.
Pentheus:
That's true, I think—at least by the right leg, on this
    side;
But on the other side the gown hangs well to the heel.
Dionysus:
You'll surely count me among your friends, when you
Witness the Maenads' unexpected modesty.

Pentheus:
Ought I to hold my thyrsus in the right hand—so,
Or in the left, to look like a Bacchanal?
Dionysus:
In the right hand; and raise it at the same time as
Your right foot. I am glad you are so changed in mind.
Pentheus:
Could I lift up on my own shoulders the whole weight
Of Mount Cithaeron, and all the women dancing there?
    (p. 225–226)

It is a symmetric and very moving dialogue in which
Dionysus and Pentheus follow the same rhythm, and we
see the process of possession, in this case, in the form of
transvestism. The kind of subtle suggestion employed by
Dionysus can be taken as a metaphor for how the
Dionysiac archetype functions in other types of possession, for example, the seduction of alcohol.

The chorus anticipates Pentheus's arrival on the
mountain. The emotional atmosphere heightens. In the
epode, with growing excitement, shouting and dancing
to the rhythm of their words, they invoke Dionysus to
appear and possess them:

Come Dionysus!
Come, and appear to us!
Come like a bull or a
Hundred-headed serpent,
Come like a lion snorting
Flame from your nostrils! (pp. 228–229)

And now a messenger comes to tell the chorus how
Agauë dismembers Pentheus:

> His mother first,
> As priestess, led the rite of death, and fell upon him.
> He tore the headband from his hair, that his wretched mother
> Might recognize him and not kill him. 'Mother,' he cried,
> Touching her cheek, 'It is I, your own son Pentheus, whom
> You bore to Echion. Mother have mercy; I have sinned,
> But I am still your own son. Do not take my life!'
> Agaüe was foaming at the mouth; her rolling eyes
> Were wild; she was not in her right mind, but possessed
> By Bacchus, and she paid no heed to him. She grasped
> His left arm between wrist and elbow, set her foot
> Against his ribs, and tore his arm off by the shoulder.
> It was no strength of hers that did it, but the god
> Filled her, and made it easy. On the other side
> Ino was at him, tearing at his flesh; and now
> Autonoë joined them, and the whole maniacal hoard.
> A single and continuous yell arose—Pentheus
> Shrieking as long as life was left in him, the women
> Howling in triumph. One of them carried off an arm,
> Another a foot, the boot still laced on it. The ribs
> Were stripped, clawed clean; and women's hands, thick red with blood,
> Were tossing, catching, like a plaything, Pentheus' flesh.
> (p. 232)

There is nothing to compare to Euripides' description of the maenads in the mountains. It is a poetic vision of the horror of an extreme state of possession, of madness, and indicative of Euripides' own Dionysiac experiences.

Archetypally, Euripides was a child of Dionysus. He was a great tragedian. It was not only the information he picked up about the Dionysiac rites (especially of the maenads on the mountain) and his stagecraft that enabled him to create such passages as those he put into the mouths of the herdsman and the messenger, it was something more, for his description of such a terrible possession seems to come from within. He seems to have accepted the contradiction in the rites that include the striking of thyrsuses on rocks to bring forth wine and milk and the tearing apart of bulls and cows. There is ample iconographic evidence of this dismemberment, *sparagmos* as it was known; it is an image of sheer horror. It is through the imagery of horror that we can connect to the hidden shadow in our nature, waiting to be discovered and to provide insight.

The description of the maenads in the mountains is not simply an anthropological imagery that belongs in a museum, nor is it merely the poetic imagination of a tragedian; it is a description of the very strange madness connecting us with unknown archaic levels of human nature. Euripides' imagination was able to bring together a very archaic ritual and tragedy, the result a real wonder.

In discussing nonhuman passion, Ruth Padel says, "Madness, supremely, is the nonhuman in the human."[97] Euripides, in the *Bacchae,* presents this nonhuman aspect of madness in an unparalleled poetic description. Poetry is the *via regia* for connecting to horror and for preparing us to read with a tragic consciousness the following passage of modern observations of animal behavior:

> Jane Goodall observed the rituals of hype in chimpanzees. In fact, as has now been captured on film, the hunting technique of chimpanzees is quite horrible. For hours, a sinister mood seems to overtake them, a conspiratorial silence. Then the mood becomes frenzied, and together—cooperatively—they encircle and close in upon some hapless monkey.

> Yelling, screaming, and shaking branches,
> they induce stark terror which, in turn, caus-
> es the prey to make mistakes. When the mon-
> key is finally caught it is torn, literally, limb
> from limb in an orgy of excitement.
> Horrendous.[98]

There is no doubt that Euripides was profoundly interested in states of possession. In *Hippolytus,* beside his excellent portrait of Aphrodite's possession of Phaedra, he brought his own list of possession. Dodds works out Euripides' list and the list of Hippocrates' *de morbo sacro:*

> Both lists include Hecate and the "Mother of
> the Gods" or "Mountain Mother" (Cybele):
> Euripides adds Pan and the Corybantes;
> Hippocrates adds Poseidon, Apollo Nomios,
> and Ares, as well as the "heroes" who are sim-
> ply the unquiet dead associated with Hecate.
> All these are mentioned as deities who *cause*
> mental trouble.[99]

Dodds notes the significance of Dionysus's absence from either list. Dionysus holds within himself a wide range of states of possession—madness, alcoholism, *duende,* and the emotions engendered by tragic Dionysiac imagery. One wonders about Euripides' life between the writing of *Hippolytus* and the *Bacchae;* the latter must have required a long brooding on the range of Dionysiac states of possession. Perhaps this variety or the ambiva- lence we have already discussed accounts for Dionysus's absence from Euripides' list.

There is an important difference between the followers of Dionysus, represented by the chorus, and Agauë. The chorus sings of the feelings of bacchants, maenads, followers of Dionysus, whose lives were devoted to the god.

O for long nights of worship, gay
With the pale gleam of dancing feet,
With head tossed high to the dewy air—
Pleasure mysterious and sweet! (p. 222)

This joy in dancing is very different from the state of those who are totally possessed by him, like Agauë at the moment she dismembers her son, Pentheus. Agauë had totally repressed Dionysus and his archetypal way of life, and so the god punished her with his madness: "I have made them bear the emblem of my mysteries" (p. 192).

It seems that a central task of culture is to know about madness. Great theater and literature has always been a reflection of human madness. In the *Bacchae,* Dionysus, the god of theater, and Dionysus, the god of madness, unite. In synthesis, the plot of the tragedy— wherein Dionysus devises the death and destruction of Pentheus at his own mother's hands—pivots on a mother killing her son because both rejected the worship of Dionysus. Euripides' tragic image can be perceived as a metaphor for reflecting the relationship between a mother and a son that ends in the most terrible destruction; in other words, it provides us with an extreme situation on which to reflect. As we have seen, Pentheus has pronounced Titanic traits: there is no religiousness in his rhetoric. His mother's envy of Semele means that she, too, denies and represses Dionysus. Titanism rules this mother/son relationship, and we need to look for what is lacking here. In repressing Dionysus, there is a brutal repression of the emotions. Dionysus took his revenge, or better said, those repressed emotions took their revenge and mother and son fell into one of the most extreme examples of destruction.

The mother/son relationship is archetypal. Within its archetypal configuration there exist all the colors of the emotional spectrum, from the white and black of positive and negative, through the endless possibilities of the many hues. Following this line of thought, the mother/son relationship between Dionysus and Semele offers a different perspective to that of Pentheus and Agauë. Semele's death before the birth of her son creates the tragic condition of a motherless child. The myth tells us that Dionysus went down into the underworld, the realm of the dead, to rescue his mother, Semele, and bring her up to heaven.[100] Psychologically, this would mean a deep consciousness of the mother/son relationship on the part of the son.

We are told also that, for this descent into the underworld, Dionysus was guided by a phallus—the phallus as pathfinder—a mystery that can only be left to a Dionysiac imagination.[101] According to tradition, Dionysus also went down into the realm of the dead and rescued Ariadne, the only woman he had loved and who had died in travail.

Euripides' *Bacchae*, written in his old age, conveys an intrinsic understanding of Dionysus and tragedy. In old age, tragedy is unavoidable. After Dionysus has meted out his punishments upon the House of Cadmus, Euripides puts Cadmus into the painful role of being his daughter's psychotherapist. It is a very moving scene, in which we see how Cadmus, through his tragic consciousness, brings Agauë to reflect on the horror of her madness and its terrible consequences:

Cadmus:

Come here. First turn your eyes this way. Look at the
    sky . . . .

Does it appear the same to you, or is it changed?

Agauë:

Yes, it is clearer than before, more luminous.

Cadmus:

And this disturbance of your mind—is it still there?

. . . and whose head is that you are holding in your arms?

. . . look straight at it. Come, to look is no great task.

    (pp. 237–238)

Agauë looks and begins to scream. Cadmus has
brought her into a full consciousness of what she has
done while possessed, and she says, "Dionysus has
destroyed us. Now I understand." I have worked out
elsewhere that the reflection of an image of horror is the
strongest therapeutic psychic mover.[102] Euripides, in a
few dramatic lines, conveys how such a reflection propitiates psychic movement. Here we have a great example
of transitional madness.[103] In the last part of the
tragedy, we see the destructive aspect of a transitory
Dionysiac madness in Agauë: the madness that destroys
her son Pentheus and changes the destiny of the House
of Cadmus.

When Cadmus has to face his terrible future of exile,
all he can say is: "Have mercy on us, Dionysus."

Thomas G. Rosenmeyer, in *The Art of Aeschylus,*
says: "In Euripidean drama, the surprise inversions of
Alcestis and *Hippolytus* and the shocking inexorabilities
of *Bacchae* leave the audience in a fruitful state of perturbation."[104] One can imagine this perturbation as a
state of *duende:* the audience tearing off their garments
as they leave the theater. I suspect that the dominant
emotions aroused by the *Bacchae* were pity for the
House of Cadmus and its destiny, and fear of Dionysus's

merciless and horrifying revenge. Euripides' religiousness was very personal. Dodds saw him as an irrationalist in contradistinction to Victorian scholars such as A. W. Verrall, who saw him as a rationalist.[105] But, for me, his soul oscillated easily between rationality and irrationality. As an image-maker, he could fashion his images with rational care or he could express just the opposite and bring forth an irrational image of such overwhelming emotional impact that it allows no margin for speculation.

The emotional climax of the tragedy was made possible by Euripides' conception of the gods' behavior as not pertaining to any rational mortal designs; it was this conception that has made him the most tragic of the tragic poets. We can learn from Euripides, for we live in times that are no longer conducive to emotional tragic consciousness. His poetry is perhaps the greatest example of rationality and irrationality paradoxically going hand in hand, expressing the wholeness of his personality. As Dionysus himself says: "Dionysus, son of Zeus, in his full nature God, most terrible, although most gentle, to mankind" (p. 222).

Notes

1. W. C. K. Guthrie, *The Greeks and Their Gods* (London: Methuen and Co., 1950), pp. 145–46.

2. Ibid., p. 145.

3. I find it confusing to see Dionysiac analogies in the outbreaks of dancing in the Middle Ages and in similar manifestations. Dionysiac rites pertain only to Dionysus, or to where there is the expression of Dionysiac culture.

4. Guthrie, *The Greeks and Their Gods,* p. 146.

5. C. E. Meier, *Healing Dream and Ritual: Ancient Incubation and Modern Psychotherapy* (Einsiedeln: Daimon Verlag, 1989).

6. Martin. P. Nilsson, *A History of Greek Religion,* trans. F. J. Fielden (Oxford: Clarendon Press, 1949), p. 215.

7. Ibid., p. 217.

8. Euripides, *Hippolytus,* trans. Philip Vellacott (Harmondsworth: Penguin Books, 1953), p. 56.

9. Rafael Lopez-Pedraza, "Sectarian and Titanic Madness in Psychotherapy," in *Mad Parts of Sane People in Analysis,* ed. Murray Stein (Wilmette, Ill.: Chiron Publications, 1993).

10. Nilsson, *A History of Greek Religion,* p. 218.

11. Ibid., p. 217.

12. Carl Kerényi, *Prometheus: Archetypal Image of Human Existence,* trans. Ralph Manheim (New York: Pantheon Books, 1963), p. 27.

13. Ibid.

14. Ibid., p. 28.

15. See Rafael Lopez-Pedraza, "Priapus," chap. 6 in *Hermes and His Children* (Einsiedeln: Daimon Verlag, 1989), pp. 175ff.

16. Kerényi, *Prometheus,* p. 37.

17. Walter Otto, *The Homeric Gods,* trans. Moses Hadas (London: Thames and Hudson, 1954), p. 33.

18. Ernst Jünger, "Gestaltwandel Eine Prognose auf das Jahr 21 Jahrhundert," *Die Zeit,* 23 July 1993 (no. 29).

19. Saint Paul is the best-known historical example of religious conversion. In his case, he brought many Jewish traits into Christianity, for example, guilt and sexual repression.

20. Aeschylus, *Prometheus Bound,* trans. Philip Vellacott (Harmondsworth: Penguin Books, 1961), p. 21. *Note:* Page numbers in text following refer to this edition.

21. See C. G. Jung, *The Collected Works,* vol. 8, *The Structure and Dynamics of the Pysche,* trans. R. F. C. Hull (London: Routledge and Kegan Paul, 1960), par. 242, where he addresses reflection as an instinct.

22. Colin Tudge, *The Day Before Yesterday: Five Million Years of Human History* (London: Jonathan Cape, 1995), p. 198.

23. I praise the classical Greeks for the way they were able to detect odd behavior: Hesiod, Aeschylus, and the Orphics, but also Homer, who began the *Iliad* with Agamemnon's odd behavior toward Achilles, his *atê,* as it was called. Such behavior is akin to what is termed psychopathic in modern psychiatry. Now we can add the evolutionist view of human opportunism and broaden our view of one of the most dangerous shadows in the complexities of the human psyche.

24. See Lopez-Pedraza, *Anselm Kiefer: The Psychology of "After the Catastrophe"* (New York: George Braziller, 1996), p. 12, for a specific discussion of inferior psychopathy; for C. G. Jung's view, see *Civilization in Transition, CW* 10, "After the Catastrophe" (London: Routledge and Kegan Paul, 1964).

25. Euripides, *Bacchae,* trans. Philip Vellacott (Harmondsworth: Penguin Books, 1973), p. 217. *Note:* Page numbers in text following refer to this edition.

26. The ritual of dismemberment was enacted in more symbolic ways than the literal and crude form described in the *Bacchae,* for example, the sacrifice and consumption of a kid. We can say that some Dionysiac elements, such as the tearing of clothes after a tragic play or the emotion of *duende,* are related to dismemberment. See Lopez-

Pedraza, "Reflections on the *Duende*," in *Cultural Anxiety* (Einsiedeln: Daimon Verlag, 1990), pp. 55ff.

27. T. S. Eliot, "The Dry Salvages," in *Four Quartets* (London: Faber and Faber, 1944), p. 29.

28. Walter Burkert, "Sacrifice, Hunting, and Funerary Rituals," part I in *Homo Nekans: The Anthropology of Ancient Greek Sacrificial Ritual and Myth,* trans. Peter Bing (Berkeley, Calif.: University of California Press, 1983).

29. See Walter Burkert, *Ancient Mystery Cults* (Cambridge, Mass.: Harvard University Press, 1987), where he traces the etymology of *teletai* as follows:

> A word family that largely overlaps with *mysteria* is *telein,* "to accomplish," "to celebrate," "to initiate"; *telesterion,* "initiation hall," and so forth. . . . Such a term becomes specific, however, when used with a personal object and with a god's name in the dative: to perform a ritual on a person for a specific god is the same as to "initiate" this person; *Dionysoi telesthenai* means to be initiated into the mysteries of Dionysus. (p. 9)

30. Carl Kerényi, *The Gods of the Greeks* (London: Thames and Hudson, 1961) pp. 145–46.

31. Homer, *Iliad,* trans. E. V. Rieu (Harmondsworth: Penguin Books, 1950), p. 120.

32. Albert Henrichs, "'He Has a God in Him': Human and Divine in the Modern Perception of Dionysus," in *Masks of Dionysus,* ed. Thomas A. Carpenter and Christopher A. Faraone (Ithaca, N.Y.: Cornell University Press, 1993), pp. 18–19.

33. Michael Jameson, "The Asexuality of Dionysus," in *Masks of Dionysus,* p. 45 n. 2; and Nonnos, *Dionysiaca,* vol. 2, book 20, trans. W. H. D. Rouse (London: William Heinemann, 1962).

34. Walter Otto, *Dionysos: Myth and Cult,* trans. Robert B. Palmer (Bloomington, Ind.: Indiana University Press, 1965), p. 102, plate 7.

35. Walter Burkert, "Bacchic *Teletai* in the Hellenistic Age," in *Masks of Dionysus,* p. 273.

36. Ruth Padel, *Whom Gods Destroy: Elements of Greek and Tragic Madness* (Princeton, N.J.: Princeton University Press, 1995), p. 101.

37. Plato, *Phaedrus and the Seventh and Eighth Letters,* trans. Walter Hamilton (Harmondsworth: Penguin Books, 1973), par. 265.

38. For a study of the psychology of creation myths, see Marie-Louise von Franz, *Creation Myths* (Dallas: Spring Publications, 1972). In most creation myths reported on by anthropology, we can see the human psyche urgently trying to create order out of chaos.

39. Euripides, *Bacchae,* edited with introduction and commentary by E. R. Dodds (Oxford: Oxford University Press, 1993), p. xvii. Dodds repeats the same lines in his appendix on maenadism in *The Greeks and the Irrational* (Berkeley, Calif.: University of California Press, 1968).

40. W. B. Stanford, "The Centrality of Emotionalism," chap. 1 in *Greek Tragedy and the Emotions: An Introductory Study* (London: Routledge and Kegan Paul, 1983).

41. See also Dodds, *The Greeks and the Irrational,* p. 185.

42. Stanford, *Greek Tragedy and the Emotions,* pp. 1–2.

43. Ibid., p. 5.

44. Euripides, *Bacchae,* p. xii.

45. E. R. Dodds, "Universal Question Mark," chap. 11 in *Missing Persons* (Oxford: Clarendon Press, 1977), pp. 97ff.

46. Padel, *Whom Gods Destroy,* p. 26, n. 16.

47. The exceptions are such scholars as E. R. Dodds, W. B. Stanford, Ruth Padel, and P. Walcot.

48. Ivan Linforth, *The Arts of Orpheus* (New York: Arno Press, 1973), p. 327. One senses that, though full of excitement, the scholarship on Dionysus tends to be romantic and cerebral, to the exclusion of the body. For this reason, Linforth's contribution is so important.

49. Tudge, *The Day Before Yesterday,* p. 252.

50. Jungian psychology of the third generation is more a given academic subject than a preparation for the inner life.

51. An experienced therapist is aware of the many cases that are unconscious of the body or, to put it more graphically, unconscious of the most common illness they might have.

52. Lopez-Pedraza, *Hermes and His Children,* pp. 19–20.

53. Euripides, *Alcestis,* trans. Philip Vellacott (Harmondsworth: Penguin Books, 1953), p. 151.

54. Martin P. Nilsson, *The Dionysiac Mysteries of the Hellenistic and Roman Age* (New York: Arno Press, 1975).

55. Burkert, *Ancient Mystery Cults,* p. 48.

56. *El Andaluz posee una sombrosa capacidad para asimilar las más disimiles influencias externas, transformarlas a la larga en autenticas manifestaciones de su propia y ancestral encrucijada de culturas.* J. M. Caballero Bonald, *Luces y sombras del flamenco* (Barcelona: Editorial Lumen, 1975), p. 23 (author's translation).

57. Regardless of whether the songs are superficial or *cante jondo,* emotion is constellated, emotion as an event. The rich variety of this music brings to mind Corybantism and the relation of a style of music to the psychology of a personality.

58. For the English reader looking for a wider view of these two art forms, on flamenco I recommend D. E. Pohren, *The Art of Flamenco* (Moron de la Frontera: Society of Spanish Studies, 1967) and on bullfighting, Ernest Hemingway, *Death in the Afternoon* (Harmondsworth: Penguin Books, 1966).

59. The animal side of Dionysus as contained by the satyrs has to be seen as a contrast to the animal aspect of madness in the discussion on Agauë's possession in the last part of Euripides' *Bacchae.*

60. See T. B. L. Webster, *The Tragedies of Euripides* (London: Methuen and Co., p. 5), where he writes: "The *Alcestis* took the place of a satyr play in 438 B.C."

61. We can find a close analogy in the black communities of Cuba in the song "El muerto se fue de rumba," meaning "the dead man who went away dancing."

62. Jane Ellen Harrison, *Prolegomena to the Study of Greek Religion* (New York: Meridian Books, 1957), p. 388.

63. Dodds, *The Greeks and the Irrational,* p. 272.

64. Niel Micklem, *On the Nature of Hysteria* (London: Routledge, 1996).

65. In this context, the animus means that the woman is acting out of the accumulated knowledge (logos) achieved by men throughout history.

66. For a Jungian perspective on the complexities of thyroid ailments, see Heinrich Karl Fierz, *Jungian Psychiatry* (Einsiedeln: Daimon Verlag, 1991), pp. 203ff, and Alfred Ziegler, "Horroris Morbus: Unit of Disease and Image of Ailing," in *The Differing Uses of Symbolic and Clinical Approaches in Practice and Theory: Proceedings of the Ninth International Congress for Analytical Psychology,* Jerusalem, 1983 (Einsiedeln: Daimon Verlag, 1986).

67. Susan Guettel Cole, "Voices from the Grave: Dionysus and the Dead," in *Masks of Dionysus,* p. 293.

68. Lopez-Pedraza, *Hermes and His Children,* p. 171.

69. Alfred Ziegler, *Archetypal Medicine* (Dallas: Spring Publications, 1983), p. 53. I see the baroque as having a strong Dionysiac ingredient, to wit, its connection to death and decay, its respect for ritual and images.

70. Kerényi, *The Gods of the Greeks,* p. 253.

71. Walter Otto, "Dionysus and the Element of Moisture," chap. 14 in *Dionysos,* pp. 160ff.

72. Ruth Padel, "The Flux of Feeling," chap. 4 in *In and Out of the Mind: Greek Images of the Tragic Self* (Princeton, N.J.: Princeton University Press, 1992).

73. Micklem, *On the Nature of Hysteria,* p. 91.

74. Thomas A. Carpenter, "On the Beardless Dionysus," in *Masks of Dionysus,* pp. 185ff.

75. Michael Jameson, "The Asexuality of Dionysus," in *Masks of Dionysus,* p. 45.

76. Twenty-three centuries later, Jung brought up the reflection of

the hero as psychopath in his "Three Essays on Contemporary Events," *CW* 10.

77. Dodds, *The Greeks and the Irrational*, p. 189.

78. Nilsson, *A History of Greek Religion*, p. 216.

79. Kerényi, *The Gods of the Greeks*, p. 255.

80. Lopez-Pedraza, "Hermes—Psychotherapy—The Hermaphrodite," chap. 1 in *Hermes and His Children*.

81. Peter Walcot, *Envy and the Greeks* (Warminster: Aris and Phillips, 1978), pp. 53ff.

82. Ibid., p. 1.

83. Kerényi, *The Gods of the Greeks*, pp. 259–260.

84. Lopez-Pedraza, *Cultural Anxiety*, p. 68.

85. These tricks of memory are easy enough to distinguish from an actual loss of memory in the medical sense, for example, the extreme condition of Alzeimer's disease.

86. T. S. Eliot, *Four Quartets*, p. 22.

87. See Stanford, *Greek Tragedy and the Emotions*, pp. 35–36.

88. When the Jesuits went to China in the sixteenth century and talked about the mystery of the Eucharist in terms of bread and wine, the Chinese had no idea what they were talking about.

89. Martin P. Nilsson, *Greek Piety*, trans. Herbert Jennings Rose (New York: W. W. Norton, 1969) and *Greek Folk Religion* (New York: Harper and Row, 1961).

90. Carl Kerényi, *Dionysos: Archetypal Image of Indestructible Life*, trans. Ralph Manheim (London: Routledge and Kegan Paul, 1976), pp. 154–155.

91. Erwin Rohde, *Psyche: The Cult of Souls and Belief in Immortality among Ancient Greeks* (1925; reprint, Chicago: Ares Publications, 1987).

92. Dodds, *The Greeks and the Irrational*, p. 271.

93. Padel, *Whom Gods Destroy*, p. 142.

94. Ibid.

95. Kerényi, *The Gods of the Greeks,* p. 258.

96. Padel, *Whom Gods Destroy*, p. 143.

97. Ibid., p. 141.

98. Tudge, *The Day Before Yesterday,* p. 197.

99. Dodds, *The Greeks and the Irrational,* p. 77.

100. In 1952, Jung was very impressed when the Catholic Church made the Virgin's bodily ascent to heaven into official dogma. He interpreted the Virgin's ascent as the feminine element completing the trinity of the Father, the Son, and the Holy Spirit into a *quaternio,* conceived of as wholeness. I see the taking of Semele to heaven by Dionysus as the archetypal background to the Christian dogma of the Virgin's bodily ascent to heaven.

101. Kerényi, *The Gods of the Greeks,* p. 259.

102. See Lopez-Pedraza, *Hermes and His Children,* pp. 57–60.

103. Padel, *Whom Gods Destroy,* pp. 76 and 101.

104. Thomas G. Rosenmeyer, *The Art of Aeschylus* (Berkeley, Calif.: University of California Press, 1982), p. 86.

105. E. R. Dodds, "Euripides the Irrationalist," in *The Ancient Concept of Progress* (Oxford: Clarendon Press, 1973), pp. 78ff.

Bibliography

Aeschylus. *Prometheus Bound*. Philip Vellacott, trans. Harmondsworth: Penguin Books, 1961.

Burkert, Walter. 1983. *Homo Nekans: The Anthropology of Ancient Greek Sacrificial Ritual and Myth*. Peter Bing, trans. Berkeley, Calif.: University of California Press.

———. 1987. *Ancient Mystery Cults*. Cambridge, Mass.: Harvard University Press.

———. 1993. "Bacchic *Teletai* in the Hellenistic Age." In *Masks of Dionysus,* Thomas A. Carpenter and Christopher A. Faraone, eds. Ithaca, N.Y.: Cornell University Press.

Caballero Bonald, J. M. 1975. *Luces y sombras del flamenco*. Barcelona: Editorial Lumen.

Carpenter, Thomas A. 1993. "On the Beardless Dionysus." In *Masks of Dionysus,* Thomas A. Carpenter and Christopher A. Faraone, eds. Ithaca, N.Y.: Cornell University Press.

Cole, Susan Guettell. 1993. "Voices from the Grave: Dionysus and the Dead." In *Masks of Dionysus,* Thomas A. Carpenter and Christopher A. Faraone, eds. Ithaca, N.Y.: Cornell University Press.

Dodds, E. R. 1968. *The Greeks and the Irrational*. Berkeley, Calif.: University of California Press.

———. 1973. *The Ancient Concept of Progress*. Oxford: Clarendon Press.

———. 1977. *Missing Persons*. Oxford: Clarendon Press.

Eliot, T. S. 1944. *Four Quartets*. London: Faber and Faber.

Euripides. *Alcestis*. Philip Vellacott, trans. Harmondsworth: Penguin Books, 1953.

———. *Bacchae*. Philip Vellacott, trans. Harmondsworth: Penguin Books, 1973.

——. *Bacchae.* Edited with introduction and commentary by E. R. Dodds. Oxford: Oxford University Press, 1993.

——. *Hippolytus.* Philip Vellacott, trans. Harmondsworth: Penguin Books, 1953.

Fierz, Heinrich Karl. 1991. *Jungian Psychiatry.* Einsiedeln: Daimon Verlag.

Guthrie, W. C. K. 1950. *The Greeks and Their Gods.* London: Methuen and Co.

Harrison, Jane Ellen. 1957. *Prolegomena to the Study of Greek Religion.* New York: Meridian Books.

Hemingway, Ernest. 1966. *Death in the Afternoon.* Harmondsworth: Penguin Books.

Henrichs, Albert. 1993. "'He Has a God in Him': Human and Divine in the Modern Perception of Dionysus." In *Masks of Dionysus,* Thomas A. Carpenter and Christopher A. Faraone, eds. Ithaca, N.Y.: Cornell University Press.

Homer. *Iliad.* E. V. Rieu, trans. Harmondsworth: Penguin Books, 1950.

Jameson, Michael. 1993. "The Asexuality of Dionysus." In *Masks of Dionysus,* Thomas A. Carpenter and Christopher A. Faraone, eds. Ithaca, N.Y.: Cornell University Press.

Jung, C. G. *The Collected Works.* R. F. C. Hull, trans. London: Routledge and Kegan Paul.

——. 1953. *Psychology and Alchemy,* vol. 12.

——. 1960. *The Structure and Dynamics of the Psyche,* vol. 8.

——. 1964. *Civilization in Transition,* vol. 10.

——. 1968. *Alchemical Studies,* vol. 13.

Jünger, Ernst. 1993. "Gestaltwandel: Eine Prognose auf das Jahr 21. Jahrhundert." *Die Zeit,* 23 July 1993 (no. 29).

Kerényi, Carl. 1961. *The Gods of the Greeks.* Norma Cameron, trans. London: Thames and Hudson.

———. 1963. *Prometheus: Archetypal Image of Human Existence.* Ralph Manheim, trans. New York: Pantheon Books.

———. 1976. *Dionysos: Archetypal Image of Indestructible Life.* Ralph Manheim, trans. London: Routledge and Kegan Paul.

Linforth, Ivan. 1973. *The Arts of Orpheus.* New York: Arno Press.

Lopez-Pedraza, Rafael. 1989. *Hermes and His Children.* Einsiedeln: Daimon Verlag.

———. 1990. *Cultural Anxiety.* Einsiedeln: Daimon Verlag.

———. 1993. "Sectarian and Titanic Madness in Psychotherapy." In *Mad Parts of Sane People in Analysis,* Murray Stein, ed. Wilmette, Ill.: Chiron Publications.

———. 1996. *Anselm Kiefer: The Psychology of "After the Catastrophe."* New York: George Braziller.

Meier, C. E. 1989. *Healing Dream and Ritual: Ancient Incubation and Modern Psychotherapy.* Einsiedeln: Daimon Verlag.

Micklem, Niel. 1996. *On the Nature of Hysteria.* London: Routledge.

Nilsson, Martin P. 1949. *A History of Greek Religion.* F. J. Fielden, trans. Oxford: Clarendon Press.

———. 1961. *Greek Folk Religion.* New York: Harper and Row.

———. 1969. *Greek Piety.* Herbert Jennings Rose, trans. New York: W. W. Norton.

———. 1975. *The Dionysiac Mysteries of the Hellenistic and Roman Age.* New York: Arno Press.

Nonnos. *Dionysiaca,* vol. 2, books 16–35. W. H. D. Rouse, trans. Loeb Classical Library. London: William Heinemann, 1962.

Otto, Walter. 1954. *The Homeric Gods.* Moses Hadas, trans. London: Thames and Hudson.

———. 1965. *Dionysos: Myth and Cult.* Robert B. Palmer, trans. Bloomington, Ind.: Indiana University Press.

Padel, Ruth. 1992. *In and Out of the Mind: Greek Images of the Tragic Self*. Princeton, N.J.: Princeton University Press.

———. 1995. *Whom Gods Destroy: Elements of Greek and Tragic Madness*. Princeton, N.J.: Princeton University Press.

Plato. *Phaedrus and the Seventh and Eighth Letters*. Walter Hamilton, trans. Harmondsworth: Penguin Books, 1973.

Pohren, D. E. 1967. *The Art of Flamenco*. Moron de la Frontera: Society of Spanish Studies.

Rohde, Erwin. 1925. *Psyche: The Cult of Souls and Belief in Immortality among Ancient Greeks*. New York: Harcourt, Brace, 1925. (Reprint. Chicago: Ares Publications, 1987.)

Rosenmeyer, Thomas G. 1982. *The Art of Aeschylus*. Berkeley, Calif.: University of California Press.

Stanford, W. B. 1983. *Greek Tragedy and the Emotions: An Introductory Study*. London: Routledge and Kegan Paul.

Tudge, Colin. 1995. *The Day Before Yesterday: Five Million Years of Human History*. London: Jonathan Cape.

von Franz, Marie-Louise. 1972. *Creation Myths*. Dallas: Spring Publications.

Walcot, Peter. 1978. *Envy and the Greeks*. Warminster: Aris and Phillips.

Webster, T. B. L. *The Tragedies of Euripides*. London: Methuen and Co.

Yates, Frances A. 1969. *The Art of Memory*. Harmondsworth: Penguin Books.

Ziegler, Alfred. 1983. *Archetypal Medicine*. Dallas: Spring Publications.

———. 1986. "Horroris Morbus: Unit of Disease and Image of Ailing." In *The Differing Uses of Symbolic and Clinical Approaches in Practice and Theory: Proceedings of the Ninth International Congress for Analytical Psychology,* Jerusalem, 1983. Einsiedeln: Daimon Verlag.